The
100-Minute
Bible
Reflections

Edited by Michael Turnbull

Publisher
The 100-Minute Press
Mystole Farm
Canterbury, Kent, CT4 7DB
United Kingdom
www.the100-minutepress.com

Title: The 100-Minute Bible Reflections

The 100-Minute Bible abridged by Michael Hinton
Reflections edited by Michael Turnbull

Contributors
Richard Ames-Lewis, John Armson
Rachel Duff, David Spriggs
Michael Turnbull

Illustrations by Helen Jenkins

First Edition 2007

ISBN Nos.
978-0-9556695-0-7

Printed by PBGroup Ltd, Sittingbourne, United Kingdom

Authors

After a career as an architect, **Richard Ames-Lewis** was called to be ordained as an Anglican priest. He has served in parish ministry for 30 years and is currently team rector of a market town and five villages in Norfolk.

John Armson started his career as a research scientist. He was then ordained as an Anglican priest in which role he served in Notting Hill, in a Cambridge college, in two theological colleges and as a cathedral canon. In retirement he lives a fairly solitary life on the edge of the Black Mountains in Herefordshire

Rachel Duff is a nurse and lives with her family in Southsea, Hampshire. They have recently returned from four years working in Indonesia. The challenges of cross cultural living, far from her roots, have encouraged her to look afresh at the Bible and the truth of the gospel message.

David Spriggs is a Baptist minister who works as an advisor on theology for the Bible Society. He is the author of several books and writes Bible reading notes for several publishers. He is married, has three children and five grandchildren. In addition to family and writing, sport, music and poetry are some of his hobbies.

Editor and writer, **Michael Turnbull** was Bishop of Rochester and then Durham. Now retired, he and his wife live in Sandwich, Kent and he is an Honorary Assistant Bishop in the Dioceses of Canterbury and Europe. As a Deputy Lieutenant of Kent he is active in the public life of Kent and travels widely as a cruise ship lecturer and chaplain.

Welcome

When the 100-Minute Bible was launched in 2005 its impact was immediate and astonishing. It was quickly amongst the best selling religious books and has been translated into over 10 different languages, including Japanese.

The Bible itself has enduring appeal but in today's world of rapid and universal communication networks, many people are looking for an accessible overview which can be read and understood in – well, 100 minutes. I have met many people, including both non-church goers and long term Christians, for whom the 100-Minute Bible has met this need. There are at least three reasons for this: first, the relevance and power of the Bible itself; second, the brilliant and reliable paraphrase provided by Michael Hinton and third, the format and presentation of the booklet which could easily fit into a pocket or handbag.

We have now attempted to build on that success by providing reflections, meditations and prayers without losing the impact of the original concept. It is our hope that this will help readers to see the relevance of the Bible to their personal circumstances and encourage them to go on exploring the Christian faith.

However, no invitation to read the Bible should be offered without a health warning. Reading the Bible can seriously damage your prejudices and intrude on those parts of your life that you would prefer to ignore. It also has the capacity to piece things together for you; to heal old wounds; to set you on new paths and bring you hope for the future. Reading these pages could be more powerful than you ever imagined.

Michael Turnbull

Editor

The Ancient World

Historic Names
(Modern Names)

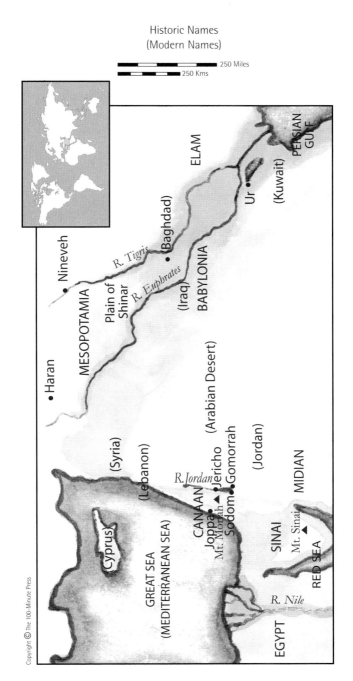

1 In the beginning

In the beginning God created heaven and earth over a period of six days. First he created light and darkness; then the vault of the heavens, separating the water above from the water below; then the dry land and all that grows in it. On the fourth day God created the sun, the moon and the stars; on the fifth the creatures of the sea and sky; and on the sixth those of the land, including humankind. On the seventh day God rested.

God made the first man, Adam, from the dust, and breathed life into him. He placed him in the beautiful and fertile garden of Eden, forbidding him to eat from the tree of the knowledge of good and evil which grew there. Because he thought man should not be alone, he created the first woman from Adam's rib; Adam named her Eve. Eve was tempted by the serpent, the most cunning of creatures; she took fruit from the forbidden tree, ate some herself, and gave some to her husband. As a punishment, God expelled them both from the garden; he condemned men to arduous toil, and woman to pain in childbearing and to submission to their husbands.

Adam and Eve bore two sons: Cain, who worked the land, and Abel, who cared for sheep. God favoured Abel's offerings over those of Cain. Cain was angry and murdered Abel; as a punishment God sentenced him to become a wanderer for ever. Adam and Eve had further children, and so the human race spread and multiplied.

In subsequent generations humankind's wickedness became more and more apparent, and God decided a fresh start was necessary. He chose Noah, the only blameless man of the time, and told him to build a boat in which he could shelter his family and living creatures of every kind. Then he sent a flood which destroyed every other living thing. When the flood receded, God sent the rainbow as a sign that he would never destroy his creation again.

After the world was repopulated, there was a time when everyone spoke the same language. People migrated to the fertile plain of Shinar between the rivers Tigris and Euphrates; there they decided to build a city named Babel, and a tower which would reach right up to heaven. To thwart them, God confused their language so that they could not understand each other, and scattered them all over the earth.

Genesis 1-11

The reality of the world in which we live

Visit an art gallery and you will find there a variety of subjects and styles. If the artists are skilled and their works have aesthetic appeal, the paintings will do two things. First they will confirm our understanding and appreciation of the world and secondly they will challenge, clarify and deepen it.

These early chapters of the Bible can be viewed like this. Through them we see the world we know, its beauty and richness as well as the place of humans in it. Both the natural world and humankind can be inspiring and also destructive. Exploring and exploiting, taking the beautiful and making it ugly, using beneficial discoveries to damage others, showing the wonder of deep human love but also our jealousy, and our power to hurt and kill.

So where does the challenge and clarification come in? The Bible displays a rich complexity with God as the main character. Creation is his – that's why it's beautiful and reliable. He made humans – that's why we have so many wonderful aspects to us. Equally, however, our tendencies for wickedness and destruction are the consequence of our trying to push God out of our lives. This broken relationship with God, which the Bible calls 'sin', distorts the whole of creation.

The early part of the Bible deals with the tough, rough world we live in, but it also offers hope. Our yearning to be back with God has not been destroyed, nor his commitment to restore us to himself. But this cannot be a cheap, or easy fix. Indeed how God woos us and works for us is the story of the rest of the Bible and how it touches our lives today.

Meditation

Care of creation is very much part of the political agenda today. What does a faith in the creator God have to contribute not only to the debate but also the action?

2 Abraham

Many generations later a man named Abram lived in Ur of the Chaldees. His family moved to Haran; then, at God's command, he journeyed south and led a nomadic life until, by agreement with his kinsman Lot, he settled on the west side of the river Jordan. Lot settled in the valley of the Jordan itself, in the city of Sodom. When fire from heaven fell on Sodom and the nearby city of Gomorrah as a punishment for their wickedness, God's intervention ensured that Lot was spared.

In due course God made a covenant (a binding agreement) with Abram, promising him a son, descendants as many as the stars in the sky in number, and possession of the whole land of Canaan. As a sign of the covenant, God renamed Abram Abraham (which means 'father of a multitude'), and he and all the males of his family were circumcised. By now he was a man of great wealth in cattle, silver and gold, but he and his wife were childless.

In their extreme old age, and by a special providence from God, Abraham and his wife Sarah bore a son, Isaac. While Isaac was still a boy, God put Abraham's faith and obedience to a supreme test. He told him to take his son and to sacrifice him at a shrine on the mount of Moriah. Abraham had reached the point of binding Isaac, laying him upon the altar, and taking a knife to slay him, when God called to him from heaven and told him to substitute a ram for his son. Abraham joyfully did so, and called the place 'The Lord will provide'.

After this Abraham sent one of his servants back to Haran to find a wife for Isaac from his wider family. At a well-side in Haran the servant met Rebecca, daughter of a nephew of Abraham. He was struck by her grace and beauty and by the hospitality her family offered him, and asked if she might be given to Isaac in marriage. She and her male relations consented, and after her journey south the marriage took place. Rebecca was childless at first, but after Abraham's death she bore twin boys, Esau first, then Jacob.

Genesis 11.27-25.26

God's invitations, his promises and his demands

The previous section ended with the world in confusion[1]. It might even appear as though God had either given up on us or lost control. But now we start to see how God is going to restore us to himself. He starts with one man, Abraham, and his family to whom he makes amazing promises but from whom he requires demanding responses. Abraham is free to choose but makes a firm commitment.

Leaving a prosperous and secure civilisation in Ur and becoming a migrant was only the start of it.

Scholars tell us that Abraham's relationship with God was very different to that in other contemporary forms of religion. At its heart was a personal relationship, not a holy place or set of rituals. Abraham was called to trust God for everything and God was able to show that his promises would come true. The gift of a son Isaac to Abraham and Sarah in their old age was part of this. But Abraham needed to learn this lesson in everyday circumstances and affirm by his free choices, including his willingness to surrender his precious son Isaac[2], that he could trust God to fulfil his promises even beyond the limitations of his own life. God promised that his descendants would in time become exceedingly numerous but, even more importantly for us, that eventually through them all peoples throughout the world would be blessed.

It was over one and a half millennia later that Jesus was born to make that promise of blessing for us available and real.

Meditation

Getting to the point where we can trust God in all things, even when it may involve the sacrifice of things we hold precious, is a long walk of faith. But it is worth asking ourselves whether there are things in our lives now which we can entrust to God for his guidance and protection.

[1] Genesis 11.1-9

[2] Genesis 15

3 Jacob and his family

When Isaac was at the point of death he asked Esau to go hunting for him, so that he could enjoy a meat meal before blessing him as his elder son. Rebecca however disguised Jacob as Esau, and tricked her husband into blessing him instead. Once given, the blessing could not be withdrawn, and Esau was furious with his brother for denying him his birthright. So, on his parents' advice, Jacob fled to Haran. On the way north he had a dream in which he saw a ladder reaching up from earth to heaven, with angels ascending and descending upon it. God revealed himself to him, and renewed the promises he had made to Abraham.

In Haran Jacob met and fell in love with Rachel daughter of Laban, his uncle. Jacob worked for Laban for seven years, on the basis of a promise that he could marry Rachel afterwards; but by trickery Laban contrived that he first married Rachel's elder sister, Leah. Jacob had to work for another seven years before he could marry Rachel. Then he in turn tricked Laban out of many of his animals and left, a wealthy man, to return to his own country. On his arrival he lavished gifts on Esau, and the two brothers were reconciled.

One day God appeared to Jacob, and gave him the new name of Israel. He told him that he would be father to a nation which would inhabit the lands promised to Abraham and Isaac. Israel had twelve sons by his wives and concubines; they were the ancestors of the twelve tribes of his people. Their names were Reuben, Simeon, Levi, Judah, Issachar, Zebulun, Dan, Naphtali, Gad, Asher, Joseph and Benjamin. Israel's favourites were Joseph and Benjamin, the sons of Rachel. Rachel died giving birth to Benjamin, the youngest.

Israel's favouritism towards Joseph angered his ten older brothers, who contrived that he should be sold as a slave into Egypt and that his father should think him dead. Joseph had a chequered career in Egypt until God enabled him to interpret Pharaoh's dreams, and secured him royal favour; he became the second person in the land, and successfully steered Egypt through a prolonged period of famine which afflicted the whole region. During this famine his brothers came to Egypt to buy food. Joseph played various tricks on them before revealing who he was. Then he obtained Pharaoh's permission for the whole family to move to Egypt, where they prospered and multiplied.

Genesis 27-50

God works through trouble and hardship

So God has launched his plan to rescue the world and it is off to a good start! But already it is clear that he is working with the very twisted material that is human beings. The Bible shows us time after time how even when people are living within the promise and protection of God, they still behave badly! Jacob cheats his brother and his father; Laban cheats Jacob; Jacob's sons sell their brother Joseph into slavery, causing harrowing grief to their father.

These stories call to mind the relational tensions, intrigues and violence that form the storylines of many novels, films and TV programmes. But, as with them, so here too, we can get involved with the characters and see something of ourselves.

There is, however, another theme running through the account of Jacob and his family. This is God's storyline of how, in spite of human waywardness, God is at work redeeming and rescuing. God's promises are working away like an antibiotic fighting infection; the promise of a growing population and prosperity - but what about the promise of a homeland?

That's where Joseph comes in. Ironically it is through Joseph's suffering that all of Jacob's family are saved from famine. Joseph is used by God to ensure that good harvests have been stored in Egypt so that both the Egyptians and all Joseph's extended family may come through this threat. Working through the web of human relationships, aspirations, deceit and occasional goodness, God is achieving his purposes. As Joseph told his brothers, God is able to bring good out of people's evil and harmful intentions. But the goodness and generosity of someone under suffering like Joseph is also required.

Meditation

Consider circumstances in personal life and in the world at large where good and positive things have emerged out of tragedy and sorrow.

Prayer

Lord God, help me, like Joseph, to start to see where you may be at work in the challenges and difficulties of my life. Please reach out and help me.   Amen

4 Moses

After the death of Joseph the Egyptians began to worry about the growing numbers of Israelites. In consequence a new Pharaoh enslaved them, and then gave instructions that all their baby boys were to be killed. To escape this edict, an Israelite mother hid her son in a reed basket by the river Nile. He was found and rescued by Pharaoh's daughter. She brought him up as her adopted son, giving him the name Moses.

One day when Moses had grown up he came across an Egyptian who was harming one of his own people; he killed him, and in consequence had to flee to the land of Midian. There God appeared to him in a burning bush, and told him that it was his mission to lead his people out of Egypt, and back to the land promised to Abraham and his descendants. At first Moses was reluctant, but eventually he and his brother Aaron went to Pharaoh to ask him to let the Israelites go. Pharaoh's first reaction was to treat the people even more harshly, so God sent a series of plagues on Egypt, culminating in one in which the firstborn child in every family died. At God's command, however, the Israelites marked the lintels of their houses with blood, and the angel of death passed over them. This deliverance was the origin of the Jewish feast of Passover.

Eventually Pharaoh gave the Israelites permission to depart; but barely had they gone when he changed his mind, and sent his army in pursuit of them. Guided by a pillar of cloud by day and a pillar of fire by night, the fugitives reached the Red Sea. At God's command Moses raised his staff and held his hand out over the sea. It parted, and the people passed through safely; but when Pharaoh's army sought to follow, the sea returned and drowned them.

Moses led the Israelites into the desert lands between Egypt and the promised land. The people were often hungry and thirsty, and complained bitterly; God fed them with a substance they called manna, and on one occasion Moses provided water by striking a rock with his staff. After defeating the Amalekites, a wandering tribe who stood in their way, they came to Mount Sinai, and camped there.

Exodus 1–19.2

8

The making of a leader

The Bible was written in an age when people were quite ready to see the hand of God working in historical events. This passage is rich in miracles, from the wonderful survival of the infant Moses, through a whole series of natural disasters, to the escape of the enslaved Israelites at the Red Sea. In the last few years, this last incident has proved the inspiration for 'liberation theology' – an approach which sees God as on the side of the down-trodden, and which actively criticises any political system which oppresses people. Needless to say, this has proved uncomfortable for some, and therefore controversial.

But as well as all these miracles, there is the no less amazing event which forged Moses into the great leader he undoubtedly became. He had hot-headedly tried to rescue a fellow Hebrew when he saw them being mistreated. That had ended in disaster. It was only later, after he received his commission from God that he was to succeed in leading the people towards the promised land. When he turned aside to see the bush which, though it was on fire, was not burnt up, he met for the first time the God of his ancestors. With this God, he proved able to lead this God's people.

When Moses asked God what he should call him, he got a curious answer[1]. God said his name was 'I AM' which is one way of saying 'I exist and am everything' It gave Moses and all who have followed him an identity too. Within the all-embracing presence of God, you are there and quite unique. It is one of the wonders of the world that there is literally no one on earth like you and you have the potential for a special relationship with God, who pervades all things and all circumstances.

Meditation

Moses presents a model of good leadership – someone who is deliberately discerning and following the will of God, someone who is focussed on the task in hand and someone who cares passionately for the people in his care. All of us have a leadership role in some sphere of our lives – home, work or leisure. Is Moses' model useful to us?

[1] Exodus 3.14

5 The giving of the Law

While the Israelites were camped at Mount Sinai God came down in fire and thunder and gave Moses the Law by which they were to live. Its moral and spiritual demands were summed up in the Ten Commandments. The people were to have no other god; they were not to make or worship images; they were not to misuse the name of God; they should keep the Sabbath day (Saturday) holy; they were to honour their parents; they were forbidden to commit murder or adultery, to steal, to give false evidence or to covet other people's possessions. Other more detailed laws governed diet, dress, personal relations, worship and every aspect of daily life.

God made a covenant with the people of Israel; he would care for them, and they would obey his commandments. This covenant was sealed with the blood from an animal sacrifice, poured out on an altar and scattered over the people. Then the leaders of the people accompanied Moses part way up the mountain and feasted before God; Moses alone ascended to the summit, and remained there for forty days.

While Moses was communing with God the people grew restless. They asked Aaron to make them gods of their own, and in response he took their golden ornaments and melted them into the form of a calf. God told Moses of this disobedience, and Moses pleaded successfully with him that he should not vent his fury on the people. However, when Moses came down from the mountain carrying God's commandments on two stone tablets and saw the people dancing before the calf, he was enraged. He shattered the tablets, ground the calf into dust, and used men of the tribe of Levi to kill many of those who had been disobedient.

Moses ascended the mountain again with two new tablets of stone. There he had a further vision of God, and received further commands. When he came down his face shone so brightly that thereafter he wore a veil when speaking to his people.

Under instruction from Moses the people created the Tabernacle which was their place of worship. Within the Tabernacle lay the Holy of Holies, a sacred space which contained the Ark of the Covenant, a wooden chest. When the Tabernacle was complete the glory of the Lord descended upon it in the form of a cloud by day and fire by night. It was only when the cloud lifted that the Israelites continued their journeying.

Exodus 19–40

A framework for living

The Jewish religion allows no pictures of God for the simple reason that he is totally 'other' from anything he has made. This rule distinguished the Jews from the people around them. But it remains a deep-seated human desire to have some kind of image, symbol, some thing around which to focus worship. Hence the tussle, described in this section, over idols.

The inspired insight of Moses – and he was uncompromisingly insistent about this – centred not on things but on behaviour as expressed in the Law. And this Law continues to be the uniting characteristic of the Jewish faith to the present day. It is about moral behaviour, but much more than that. The Law reflects the holiness of God: his otherness. It provides opportunities in the mundane things of everyday living, to be like God: holy, just and merciful.

The Law then was an insight into the Jewish understanding of God. It was also a practical framework for living. Moses and the people needed it. In the space of only forty years they went through profound cultural change from nomadic animal husbandry towards a settled farming community, from slaves to land owners, from a wandering tribe towards a political nation. The social organisation of a large group of people undergoing such changes raised huge questions about the rules under which they operated.

The Ten Commandments of the Law provided that framework for they are applicable to human being beings wherever they are and whatever their circumstances. Without conformity to them any society will eventually collapse. What God gave to Moses on Mount Sinai has been a gift to the world.

For the Jewish people, obedience to the Law was everything, for the Law revealed the holiness and justice of God. The reading of the Law became central to Jewish worship. Jesus' own summary of the Law, love God and love your neighbour as yourself, is a core belief of Christians throughout the world.

Meditation

The first four commandments are about our relationship to God and the last six about our relationship to each other. Many think there is a link between the decline of a society and its rejection of the basic framework for living which the Ten Commandments offer. Is there evidence of this today?

6 Joshua and the Judges

Moses led the Israelites for forty years. Eventually they came to the east bank of the river Jordan, where Moses died and Joshua succeeded him. God held back the waters of the river so that the Israelites could cross it and lay siege to the city of Jericho. For six days their army marched round the city. On the seventh they marched round it seven times; and, as the trumpets blew and the soldiers shouted, the walls of the city collapsed. The Israelites advanced into it and put the inhabitants to the sword.

In subsequent years Joshua conquered much of the promised land. Killing or enslaving many of the existing inhabitants, he settled eleven of the twelve tribes on their own land. The Levites, the priestly tribe, lived in the towns.

After Joshua's death there was no single leader of the Israelites for many years.   Individual tribes conducted campaigns to enlarge their territories, and were often seduced into worship of the gods of the peoples among whom they lived. God punished them through defeat in battle; when they repented, he raised up 'Judges' (military and political leaders) who delivered them from their enemies. This cycle of events repeated itself over a long period.

One notable Judge was named Gideon. He raised an army against an invasion by hostile tribes, but then dismissed most of his followers. He equipped the three hundred who remained with clay jars, torches and trumpets, and attacked the enemy camp by night. His soldiers surrounded the camp, smashed the jars which held the lighted torches, blew their trumpets, and shouted: 'A sword for the Lord and for Gideon'. Panic-stricken, the enemy began fighting among themselves, and were slaughtered as they fled.

Samson, another Judge, who was under a vow and forbidden to cut his hair, was a man of immense strength, who once killed a lion with his bare hands. He was in constant conflict with the Philistines, who lived to the west of the Israelites. Eventually he was captured through the treachery of Delilah, a woman with whom he was infatuated; she cut off his hair and his strength left him. The Philistines blinded and enslaved Samson; but, as his hair grew again, his strength returned. At a festival Samson was brought to the temple of the god Dagon so that the Philistines could mock him. He put his arms round the central pillars of the temple and dislodged them. The building collapsed; Samson was killed, and a multitude of Philistines with him.

Deuteronomy 34; Joshua; Judges

Commitment to God and to each other

Moving home is rarely as easy as we expect. Even with the best of planning many unexpected events happen, the furniture removers are delayed, the people haven't finished moving out when we arrive, the central heating won't work and all the boxes end up in the wrong rooms! It is easy for tempers to become frayed!

Imagine what it was like arriving in the land promised by God after forty years wandering. Yes, they had new laws; yes, they had a new leadership structure, yes, they had had time to get to know one another and become more organised; but Moses was dead, the present inhabitants were often far from welcoming and it wasn't long before the previous commitments of the Israelites to the Law of God began to wear thin.

Through the covenant with God there were two levels of commitment, first to God and then to each other. The stories of the Judges lead to the conclusion that as the people felt more secure they started to weaken their relationship of loyalty to God. Then their commitments to support each other across tribal boundaries seemed less valid – why should they risk themselves for the 'others'? Then disaster struck. In their need, they turned back to God who, at the appropriate times, called leaders, Judges, to bring them freedom. This cycle of oppression and rescue, triggered by the Israelite's rebellion against God and his standards, seems unbreakable. This raises the profound possibility that God will eventually say 'No' when they appeal for help! What on earth can be done? By the end of the era of the Judges anarchy is looming, as each person does what seems right to them.

Meditation

If you were God would you lose patience with such unreliable people? How might God see us, individually and as communities?

The territories of the twelve tribes

12 TRIBES OF ISRAEL
NEIGHBOURING TRIBES
Historic Names
(Modern Names)

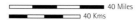
40 Miles
40 Kms

(Lebanon) ARAMEANS

HITTITES

Damascus •

Sidon •

Mt. Hermon ▲

(MEDITERRANEAN SEA)

SIDONIANS

GREAT SEA

(Syria)

NAPHTALI

ASHER

Sea of Galilee

Mt. Carmel ▲ **ZEBULUN**

ISSACHAR

Mt. Gilboa ▲

M A N A S S E H

Samaria •

R. Jordan

GAD

AMMONITES

(Tel-Aviv) • Joppa

• Shiloh

EPHRAIM

DAN

BENJAMIN • Jericho

(Jordan)

Kiriath-jearim •

• Jerusalem

• Bethlehem

REUBEN

PHILISTINES

• Hebron

• Gaza

JUDAH

Dead Sea

MOABITES

SIMEON

EDOMITES

Joshua 13–21

Copyright © The 100-Minute Press

15

7 Samuel, Saul and David

During the time of the Judges a childless woman called Hannah went to pray at a shrine named Shiloh, served by the priest Eli. She promised that, if she were granted a child, she would dedicate him to God. Soon afterwards she bore a son whom she named Samuel; when he was of an age to leave home, she gave him to serve God in the shrine. One night God called him. At first Samuel thought Eli was summoning him, but Eli realised what was happening, and instructed him that when the call came again he was to say: 'Speak, Lord, your servant is listening'. He spoke as commanded, and was given the message that Eli's sons were unworthy of the priestly office.

In manhood Samuel became Judge over all Israel. He called his people back to the worship of God, and led them to victory in battle over the Philistines. However his sons, like Eli's, proved unworthy to succeed him, and agitation grew for a king. Samuel warned the people that a king would exploit them for his own purposes and would weaken their reliance on God; but they persisted in their demand. So Samuel selected a young man named Saul from the tribe of Benjamin, and anointed him as King.

Saul quickly proved himself as a military leader, as did his son Jonathan; but they had a hard task maintaining themselves against the Philistines, and Saul angered Samuel by disobeying God's commands. Samuel therefore looked for another king, and secretly anointed David, the youngest son of Jesse of Bethlehem, from the tribe of Judah.

Saul was frequently attacked by an evil spirit. So, because David was a skilled musician, he was summoned to the court to play to him and to rescue him from rage and melancholy. David achieved a wider fame when he overcame the giant Goliath, a Philistine champion, killing him with a stone from a sling. He became a successful military leader and a close friend of Jonathan; he was given a daughter of Saul in marriage.

Saul however grew jealous of David, and plotted to kill him; but with Jonathan's help David escaped. He became an outlaw, constantly on the run, and eventually took service with the Philistines. He was not however with them at the battle of Gilboa, at which the Israelites were defeated and both Saul and Jonathan were killed. These deaths cleared the way for David to claim the throne.

1 Samuel

The building of a nation

Leadership is always a thorny issue. Outstanding men and women, picked to lead, often get big-headed, feather their own nest, and let down the people who chose them. One of the interesting things about the Bible is the different styles of leadership it reveals. Military leaders, great kings, charismatic individuals lead up to the distinctive servant leadership of Christ.

When the people fled out of Egypt about 1300 BC, 'Israel' was still a loose association of 12 tribes. As they moved into the promised land, hostility from surrounding peoples made it politically sensible to become a confederation. This needed a new kind of leadership, and inevitably charismatic individuals arose, whose valour and wisdom together with an ability to know how and when to fight commended them. Such men were then generally recognised as leaders.

These leaders were known as 'Judges' – though clearly not judges in our modern sense. As well as being warriors, they were also called upon to decide thorny legal or moral issues which arose in one tribe or another. This arrangement survived for about four centuries.

Thus the building blocks of a nation were put in place: a land with boundaries to defend, relative economic stability, a legal and moral framework for living with justice, a well tried faith with a distinctive vocation in the world and now a succession of leaders whom the surrounding nations would come to admire. After the Judges, kings Saul, David and Solomon lead the emergence of a significant power in the known world.

Meditation

As in the story of Eli and Samuel, the calling of the nation by God gave to it a sense of purpose and destiny. To what extent in today's world do we see individuals and nations claiming a call by God and what does this say about their integrity and effectiveness?

Prayer

O Lord God, just like Samuel, keep my mind open to hearing your call.   Amen.

8 David as King

David claimed Saul's crown with the support of the southern tribes of Judah and Benjamin, but it was only when he had defeated Saul's heirs that he was acknowledged as king by the northern tribes. After some years he captured the city of Jerusalem and made it his capital. He knew by now that God had confirmed him as King and had made him powerful so that he could govern the whole Israelite community. To make Jerusalem the centre of religious worship, and to ensure the loyalty of the northern tribes, he brought the Ark to Jerusalem from its previous resting-place at Kiriath-jearim. God told him through Nathan the prophet that he was to leave building a temple to house the Ark to his successor.

In a series of wars David defeated surrounding peoples and expanded the boundaries of his kingdom from Egypt to the Euphrates. He proved himself as a statesman and administrator as well as a military leader, and was famous for his skill as a poet and musician. However, despite his deep religious faith, he disgraced himself by falling in love with Bathsheba, a married woman, and by contriving to have her husband, Uriah, killed in battle. He was severely rebuked by Nathan for marrying Bathsheba, and the first son of their marriage died. Their second son was Solomon.

David had a number of sons by other marriages. His immediate heir, Amnon, was killed by his own half-brother, Absalom, because he had raped Absalom's sister. After a period of disgrace Absalom was allowed back into the King's favour. This did not however prevent him from plotting a rebellion which was supported by the northern tribes, and which was initially successful. David was forced to flee from Jerusalem, but Absalom mishandled his opportunities, and was defeated in a battle fought soon afterwards. Against David's instructions, and much to his distress, Joab, the commander of his army, killed Absalom.

In the last period of his forty-year reign David consolidated his hold on his kingdom. In extreme old age he grew feeble, and his eldest surviving son Adonijah conspired with Joab, intending to claim the succession. However Bathsheba had secured a promise from David that Solomon should become King; and, with the support of Nathan and other powerful dignitaries, she persuaded him to proclaim Solomon publicly. After succeeding to the throne Solomon had all the chief conspirators against him put to death.

2 Samuel; 1 Kings 1-2

The fallible character of a great leader

King David was an outstanding man of many gifts; yet his life was full of contradictions. Handsome and loveable, yet fallible and ruthless; a tender musician but a man of war; of indomitable will, often magnanimous; strong, yet not afraid to weep penitential tears in public. He could be both a rebel and an establishment figure par excellence; a giant-killer and a home-builder. David remains one of the outstanding characters of this era.

Under David's strong and politically shrewd centralising leadership, the twelve tribes of Israel grew into a single nation. He established a new, national, capital: Jerusalem, which became known as 'the city of David'. He consolidated his choice by bringing the religious centre of Israel there, so that it also became known as 'Zion, city of God.' But he made mistakes and paid for them: God did not allow him to build the Temple. (That was to fall to his son, Solomon: see section 10.) He was not perfect: his adultery was severely criticised by the prophet Nathan, who told David, in a subtle and penetrating way, a story about a rich man stealing a poor man's lamb. David denounced the rich man – and by analogy he condemned himself.

David's overbearing manner eventually made enemies and led to political division: even his own son turned against him. Yet David built a kingdom – an empire, indeed – which stretched from Egypt to north of Syria. He put Israel on the map as never before.

Long after this death, Israel looked back to those great days. For the first followers of Christ, David's 'line' and succession lent authenticity to the claims of Jesus to be the Messiah. He was to be the one who would rule in a newly-established Kingdom. When the crowds welcomed Jesus into Jerusalem on the first Palm Sunday, they sang 'Hosanna to the Son of David'.

Meditation

What should a nation look for in its leaders? What should we expect from our Christian leaders? In our own leadership roles – at home, at work, at play – do we follow the best or the worst of David's examples?

9 The Psalms

Psalms were the hymns of the Jewish people. Because David was noted as a composer his name was attached to many of them, but they actually came from a number of pens over a long period. They were primarily intended for use in public worship, and especially for the great festivals at Jerusalem. They were sometimes sung to a secular tune and often to an instrumental accompaniment by the people as a whole or by a choir of Levites (the servants of the Temple) with the people responding 'Hallelujah' ('Praise God') or 'Amen' ('So be it').

Psalm 150 paints a vivid picture of Israel at worship:

> Praise God in his holy place:
> praise Him in the firmament of heaven.
>
> Praise Him for his mighty deeds:
> praise Him in his surpassing greatness.
>
> Praise Him in the sound of the trumpet:
> praise Him on harp and lyre.
>
> Praise Him with tambourines and dancing:
> praise Him with strings and pipe.
>
> Praise Him with clanging cymbals:
> Praise Him with loud cymbals.
>
> Let everything that has breath: praise the Lord.

Psalms were of various kinds: hymns of praise, laments, thanksgivings, or meditations. Several were intended for royal occasions, such as a coronation or a wedding. Some were sung at the daily Temple burnt offering, some by pilgrims on their way to and from Jerusalem, some at the Passover festival. Some expressed rage and hatred. Between them they represented the whole range of Jewish spirituality.

Psalm 23 is an expression of communion with God:

> The Lord is my shepherd: I shall not want.
>
> He makes me lie down in green pastures:
> he leads me beside still waters.
>
> He restores my spirit: he leads me in the paths of righteousness for his name's sake.
>
> Even though I walk through the valley of the shadow of death, I will fear no evil: for you are with me: your rod and staff comfort me.
>
> You prepare a table before me in the presence of my enemies: you anoint my head with oil; my cup runs over.
>
> Surely goodness and mercy shall follow me all the days of my life: and I shall dwell in the house of the Lord for ever.

Inspiration in poetry, touching all aspects of life

'A card for every occasion'! Go into any large card shop and we are offered cards for an amazing variety of situations – any birthday we like, of course, but also weddings, funerals, exams, house moves, Mothering Sunday, and dozens of others.

It is easy to think of the Psalms as a card shop. Yes, we could send our own words for the sad bereavement or the young person's examination, but we can also choose a ready-made card which is 'just right'. The Psalms express most human emotions from despair to triumph, from grief to anger, from sorrow to joy. There are hymns and prayers, personal reflections and communal ones. Some of them deeply question how God reacts, expressing our human perplexities and confusion; others exude a growing confidence in God and some do both, plotting a journey into a more robust and mature faith. As in a card shop, through metaphor, image and words there is in the Psalms something to make everyone of us feel that there is something here for us.

Here are just a few samples:

Feeling lonely

> The Lord is my shepherd I shall not want[1]

Sensing danger

> I have set God always before me

> With him at my right hand I cannot be shaken[2]

Delighting in God

> The Lord is good and his love is everlasting

> His truth is reliable and lasts for ever[3]

Struggling with guilt

> Be merciful to me O God.....wash away all my evil[4]

Of course, as with the card we choose, there is always room to add our own personal thoughts or wishes towards God. The fact that others produced them does not mean they won't help us. Why not try them?

Continued

When people find that words cannot fully express something they feel deeply, they will often turn to poetry or art or music. It is worth reflecting on the variety of ways in which the truth of God might touch our hearts and influence our actions.

Prayer – based on part of Psalm 139

Father God, thank you that you cared for me when I was growing in my mother's womb and that you still lovingly watch over me always.   Amen

[1] Psalm 23

[2] Psalm 16

[3] Psalm 100

[4] Psalm 51

10 Solomon and the division of his Kingdom

Early in his reign King Solomon had a dream in which God appeared to him and offered him anything he wanted. Because Solomon chose wisdom God was pleased with him, and promised him wealth and glory as well. Solomon did indeed become famous for his wisdom: for the proverbs and songs he composed, and for his knowledge of the natural world. He was a wise administrator of justice too. On one occasion two women came before him, each claiming that a baby boy was her own. Solomon called for a sword and offered to cut the boy in two, giving half to each claimant. One of the women agreed; the other said she would prefer her rival to have the living child. She, the king decided, was the real mother.

Solomon built himself a splendid palace in Jerusalem. He also built and lavishly furnished a Temple, which held the Ark and which became the centre of the worship and sacrificial practice of the Israelite religion. When the Queen of Sheba in Arabia came to visit Solomon she was dazzled by the spectacle of his court.

However splendour came at a price. To support the vast expense of his rule Solomon imposed forced labour and heavy taxation on his people, and bartered away some of the territory which David had acquired. Nor was he wholly faithful to the Israelite religion. Influenced by his many foreign wives and concubines, he built shrines for, and even worshipped, gods other than the God of Israel.

Solomon had to deal with opposition both from outside and within his kingdom. In the later years of his reign he was harassed by the rulers of neighbouring countries, and he had to quell an attempt at rebellion by Jeroboam, one of his courtiers.

When Solomon died his son Rehoboam succeeded him, but Jeroboam returned from exile to confront him. The northern tribes had been harshly treated under Solomon and they sought a promise that their burdens would be lessened. Rehoboam replied however: 'My little finger is thicker than my father's loins. My father whipped you but I shall flay you'. At once the northern tribes rebelled, choosing Jeroboam as their king. Rehoboam was left only with the southern territory of Judah. There was constant war between the two kingdoms, and in both pagan gods were widely worshipped.

1 Kings 3-14

The rise and fall of a great king

Politics can be a dirty business and being a politician in our tough world without becoming corrupted is not always easy. The story of Solomon fits into this pattern. Even with the wisdom of God and a desire to honour God Solomon failed, in the end.

There were fundamentally three kinds of pressure that Solomon had to cope with. There was pressure from within his Kingdom which in the end meant that people were, or certainly felt they were, being treated unfairly, especially those far away from the capital city, paying a disproportionate cost for the limited benefits they received. The second pressure was from without – forming alliances with other nations can provide protection from external threats, but usually involves both obvious and more subtle compromises. These eventually broke the heart of the nation. Thirdly there are the personal pressures which revealed weaknesses in the leader. Like so many leaders, Solomon was susceptible to fame, power and lust!

The result was a time-bomb which exploded when he died; not only a divided nation but also a weakened one. The renewed focus on God which had been at the heart of Israel's early kings and their nation-building was faltering. In the end, it was not the leaders alone who suffered, but the whole nation. This was to be Israel's experience for many centuries.

Meditation

We all have to live in a tough world and most of us have to cope with similar pressures, even if they are scaled down in intensity. You may wish to ask yourself questions about your own situation and responses. If we seek God with integrity he will be there for us.

Prayer – based on part of Psalm 139

O God, test me and discover my thoughts. Find out if there is any evil in me and show me how to deal with it.   Amen

11 Elijah and Elisha

From the reign of Jeroboam onwards the northern Kingdom of Israel had a chequered and bloodthirsty history. Disputes over the succession often resulted in the wholesale massacre of the families of the defeated contenders.

King Ahab, whose father Omri had fought his way to the throne, succeeded to it in about the year 869 BC. Elijah the prophet condemned him because, influenced by his wife Jezebel, he worshipped the Canaanite god Baal. Elijah prophesied that God would punish Ahab with a drought. When it occurred Elijah took refuge by a stream and was fed by ravens. When the stream dried up he was cared for by a widow. He repaid her hospitality by miraculously replenishing her scanty stock of flour and oil, and by bringing her son back to life after he had died.

Then Elijah challenged the prophets of Baal to meet him on Mount Carmel. to see who could bring an end to the drought. The prophets of Baal tried to bring rain by dancing, self-mutilation and sacrifice, but failed. Then Elijah successfully called on God to send down fire from heaven to consume a sacrifice, and prayed for rain. It came at once; but, since Elijah had incited the people to kill the prophets of Baal, he had to flee. He came to Mount Horeb and there had a direct experience of God: not in the wind, earthquake and fire which came down on the mountain, but as an almost inaudible voice, a sound of gentle stillness. God told him to name Elisha as his successor.

Some time later Ahab tried to acquire the vineyard of a man called Naboth. Naboth refused to sell, so, on the advice of Jezebel, Ahab arranged for him to be falsely accused and stoned to death. Ahab confiscated the vineyard, and was strongly condemned by Elijah for his wickedness.

Eventually Ahab was killed in battle, and was succeeded in turn by his sons Ahaziah and Jehoram. During the reign of Ahaziah Elijah was taken up to heaven in a chariot of fire. Elisha proved himself a worthy successor by performing miracles. Most spectacularly, he cured Naaman, commander of the King of Aram's army, of leprosy. Elisha refused to speak to Naaman in person, but sent a message that he was to wash himself seven times in the river Jordan. Naaman was indignant at this dismissive treatment, but eventually agreed to do as he had been told. His leprosy left him.

1 Kings 15 - 2 Kings 5

Religion and politics

Kings and prophets are two strands running through the history books of the Bible, as tightly bound as the strands of the DNA double helix. Kings had the task of government and, although divinely chosen, often got bogged down in the mire of intrigue and favours due. Alongside them – or, as often, opposing them – were prophets, the eccentrics, the outsiders; driven men who frequently spoke out against the corruption they saw in high places. They were the investigative journalists of their day and were fuelled by a keen sense of God's own passionate love and justice. They saw with the eyes of God, behind the scenes of history, behind human shenanigans, and were often chased out of human society for doing so. This tension, then as now, could be creative and sustaining.

To us, some of the stories may read like magic, and seem rather far-fetched – fire falling from heaven on Elijah's sacrifice, chariots ascending in a whirlwind and so on. We should not dismiss these stories but look for the hidden meaning amongst the imagery. There are also some very human stories. The tale of Naboth's vineyard could come out of today's newspapers – greed, sleaze and murder are all there. Likewise Naaman's pride and snobbery eventually had to give way if he wanted to be healed – physically, psychologically and spiritually. So often in the Bible body, mind and spirit are seen as a whole. When one part of us is hurt, it affects all the other parts.

Meditation

Bishop Desmond Tutu once said that anyone who believes that religion and politics should not be linked has not read the same Bible as he has. This period of Biblical history shows the strength of that argument. Private and public morality is inextricably bound together. Beneath the history it is possible to see religious truths developing, revealing themselves over the centuries – a process which still continues. Can you think of examples?

Prayer

Lord, make me as passionate as you are to see justice and honesty in our public life. Help me to take my opportunities to see that fairness and truth prevail.   Amen

12 The northern Kingdom's downfall; Isaiah

Elisha took vengeance on the family of Ahab by arranging for Jehu, one of Jehoram's generals, to be anointed king. After being anointed Jehu drove furiously to the town of Jezreel and murdered Jehoram. Jezebel was thrown from an upper window and her corpse eaten by dogs. All descendants of Ahab and the leading worshippers of Baal were murdered. Baal worship was stamped out, but other forms of idolatry continued.

Jehu and his descendants reigned over the northern Kingdom for many years, but eventually his dynasty too was overthrown. The kingdom had an unsettled history, sometimes prospering and sometimes being defeated by neighbouring peoples. At a time of relative prosperity the prophet Amos fiercely criticised the exploitation of the poor by the rich, and the prophet Hosea attacked Israel's unfaithfulness to her loving God. Both prophets taught that God valued compassion and social justice above religious rituals.

In the 8th century BC Assyria became the predominant power in the region. For a time the northern Kingdom survived by pursuing pro-Assyrian policies; but eventually an attempt to throw off the Assyrian yoke resulted in the siege of the capital Samaria and its capture in the year 721 BC. Many citizens were deported, and the northern Kingdom ceased to exist.

Meanwhile the southern Kingdom of Judah had a less turbulent history. For the most part it was ruled by descendants of David; often they worked closely with the priests of the Temple, and tried, though without total success, to do away with pagan worship. Like the northern Kingdom, Judah was forced to pay tribute to Assyria; a defiant alliance with Egypt provoked an invasion and a siege of Jerusalem which the monarchy was fortunate to survive. The prophet Isaiah, who lived at this time, attacked the vices of the rich and powerful, and advocated a policy of neutrality rather than one of entering into alliances hostile to Assyria. He prophesied the coming of the Messiah, a descendant of David who would rule in justice and mercy over a restored Israel.

King Josiah, who reigned in the first part of the 7th century BC, reformed religious practice. The contents of a scroll discovered in the Temple in Jerusalem provided the basis for a return to purity of worship and behaviour. Religious sites dedicated to other gods were destroyed and the importance of the Temple enhanced. However Josiah was defeated and killed when he tried to prevent an Egyptian invasion, and his reforms proved to be short-lived.

2 Kings 8 - 23.30; Amos; Hosea; Isaiah 1 - 39

Prophets present the choices

What are the most powerful forces at work in the world? Some would say economics, others would say military, and still others might choose less obvious things such as culture and language. In Elisha's time it often seemed to the political leaders that military power, especially that of their brutal neighbour, Assyria, was the main power to negotiate with in order to protect their people. It certainly was a force to be reckoned with and once it decided to campaign southwards it was hard to resist. In the end in spite of various political manoeuvres the northern kingdom fell to them.

The prophets - people such as Amos, Hosea and Isaiah - saw matters differently. They believed that being loyal to God was the most important factor in the kingdom's safety. That loyalty included the ways the people worshipped, such as not getting involved with the fertility gods and goddesses who promised material prosperity but involved sexual impurity. Loyalty also involved building a community based on social justice and practical care and excluding dishonest business practices and corrupt justice systems. They believed that keeping a strong and mutually committed community was the best way to survive, because this was God's will.

Interestingly, archaeology has brought to light from almost 3,000 years ago, evidence of Assyria's architectural strength, political organisation and military might. But it doesn't take archaeology to prove that what also survived from that age was the vision of God that the prophets had and their testimony to the reality of God in ordinary life and His impact on history. Their words have been a living tradition, renewing national cohesion and morality time and time again.

Meditation

So, what really are the strongest forces in our world? What features of politics and morality contribute to the survival of a healthy society?

We may ask the same question about our personal lives. What are the things which really give us energy and motivation? Making money is a major motivation for many people. Status and recognition is more important for others. But does that kind of ambition really allow us to live at peace with ourselves?

Continued

Prayer

Father God, encourage in our time the forces that build up rather than destroy all that is good and creative in the world.

Begin with me and kindle within me the kind of motivations and ambitions which work for the common good.   Amen

13 Jonah

The story of Jonah is set at a time when the empire of Assyria was at its height. God commanded the prophet Jonah to go to the Assyrian capital of Nineveh, to condemn its people for their wickedness. To escape this command, and to put himself (as he hoped) out of God's reach, Jonah boarded a ship going from Joppa to Tarshish. But during the journey God sent a great storm. The sailors prayed to their gods and threw things overboard to lighten the ship. Still fearing for their safety, they cast lots to discover who was to blame for their misfortune. The lot fell on Jonah, who confessed that he had been trying to escape the true God who had made heaven and earth. He suggested that the crew throw him overboard, and, having tried in vain to reach the land, they did so; at once the storm subsided. Jonah was swallowed by a great fish, and spent three days inside it before being cast up on the shore.

Realising the folly of disobedience, Jonah obeyed a second command from God: he went to Nineveh and prophesied its destruction. King and people alike accepted his message; they repented, fasted, and clothed themselves and their animals in sackcloth. Consequently God withheld his punishment of them. Jonah was very angry because his prophecy had been set aside, and reproached God for his compassion and generosity. He went outside the city, took shelter in the shade of a bush which God provided, and sulked.

The next day God struck the bush and it withered. Jonah was exposed to the full heat of the sun and to a scorching wind; he was so overcome that he prayed for death. God asked him if he was angry that the bush had withered. Jonah replied that he was furious; to which God responded: 'If you are so upset about a bush which came up one day and died the next, am I not entitled to be sorry for the 120,000 people of Nineveh in their ignorance and helplessness?'

Jonah

Holding up a mirror to ourselves and the world

If satire or irony is your choice, you will probably feel at home with the story of Jonah. But equally if you like a good story you will also lap this up. At the heart of it is the challenge to all who believe they are better than others or to those who like to draw boundaries to keep people out.

At every turn Jonah is shown to be a less godly man than he thinks he is. He prides himself on his obedience to God. But as soon as God wants to send him on a challenging errand, he can't tolerate it and seeks to hide from God. Of course, if God is the Lord of the Universe as Jonah's creed proclaimed, he should have realised the futility of this venture, but he still flees. Soon Jonah's faith is portrayed as weak compared with the pagan sailors. It is they who have to stir Jonah to pray. It's not only their faith but their compassion which puts Jonah in a bad light. They are willing to risk their lives to try and protect him; only as a last resort do they cast him overboard.

And so the implicit derogatory comparisons continue as Jonah ends up preaching for God in Nineveh and furious with God that his pagan, hard-hearted, evil audience respond wholeheartedly to God and turn from their wicked ways. God's care for the whole world shows up Jonah's narrow faith.

Jonah is an example that one of the dangers of religion is being so concerned with detail that we fail to see the big picture. Rather like an artist who is painting a huge mural and so concentrates on one corner that he fails to see the whole. What he is working at therefore loses its perspective.

Meditation

Looking too long in a mirror may not be healthy or edifying! However some self-examination is important to make sure we are becoming what we hope to be and to correct any negative attitudes which may, even unconsciously, be taking a hold on us. Some people seek the help of a trusted friend who can help them to look at the whole picture of their lives and their place within God's plans.

Prayer

O God, please save me from self-deception, help me to be truthful about myself. Give me the courage to change what is negative within in me. Amen

14 The southern Kingdom's downfall; Jeremiah

King Josiah's defeat at the hands of Pharaoh Necho resulted in the imposition of a puppet monarchy in the southern Kingdom of Judah, and in the payment of tribute. Egypt was however unable to protect Judah from the increasingly powerful empire of Babylon, which replaced Assyria as the dominant power in the region. Judah became a satellite state to Babylon; then, after a revolt, the Babylonians besieged Jerusalem, captured it in 597 BC and took away King Jehoiachin and large numbers of leading citizens to captivity in Babylon. A few years later the puppet King Zedekiah whom the Babylonians had installed also revolted. After a second siege, Jerusalem was taken again, its walls and the Temple destroyed, and more of the population deported. A third revolt, in which the Babylonian Governor of Judah was murdered, also failed, and its leaders fled into Egypt.

When they fled they took with them the prophet Jeremiah, the greatest religious figure of his age. He came from a priestly family, but in his teaching he had fiercely attacked the presumption that the Temple in Jerusalem guaranteed the city's safety. He had also attacked the King and his entourage for the social injustices which they permitted and perpetrated. With regard to foreign policy, he had advocated neutrality between Egypt and Babylon, and, later, submission to Babylon as the least damaging courses of action to follow. In a letter to the exiles in Babylon he had urged them to seek peace for themselves and for the city in which they now lived.

Jeremiah had a deep sense of God, and a personal but agonising relationship with Him. Much of his teaching was concerned with sin and judgment, and only occasionally did he look forward to happier times to come. He was deeply unpopular with his own people, and suffered greatly at their hands. His advice was scoffed at and ignored; some of his prophecies, which had been written down by the scribe Baruch, were burned by the King in person; he was beaten and placed in the stocks; during the siege of Jerusalem he was imprisoned and for a time cast into a muddy pit. His enforced exile in Egypt was the final episode in a life full of tragedy but also of inspired teaching and dogged faithfulness.

2 Kings 23.29-26; Jeremiah

The nature of true success

How do you measure success? Truly significant success, greatness as we might also call it, is often not obvious during the person's lifetime. Think of great innovators, musicians and artists. Often they were deeply unhappy people and experienced rejection and misunderstanding. They often received no financial rewards in their lifetimes, even though now their work sells for enormous sums of money. Frequently, if you are really great, success arrives late.

This is true of Jeremiah. He struggled in his relationship with God; he was intensely lonely; his insights were rejected and he suffered deeply because he could see what devastation was coming to his nation and he couldn't stop the folly that would take it there. Yet to him were granted two privileges.

First when Jerusalem was captured by the Babylonians and many of the elite were exiled there, God gave Jeremiah the task of encouraging them to believe that life with and for God was still possible in a foreign land, but also that there would be a return. In other words he provided both help to survive the present purposefully and hope that, at least for their children, there could be a new life.

Secondly, to Jeremiah was given the vision of a more distant day when God would make a new arrangement with humankind. This is one of the central themes of the Bible and is often referred to as the new covenant. Christians believe that Jesus came to fulfil this. It describes how the relationship with God will be primarily individual and personal. It is not about organisations or status but more about a family life of the community where all things are built on mutual trust. God, in his generosity, takes the initiative and gives strength and confidence to help the people make a response. In this and other ways, Jeremiah pointed forward to the new relationship with God that Jesus would bring about 600 years later. Now that is true success.

Meditation

When we get to end of our lives, how will we measure our success? How does the answer to this affect our present ambitions?

What are the features of a personal relationship with God?

15 Exile and return

The people from the southern Kingdom who had been deported to Babylon were not badly treated, and some of them prospered. They had however to rethink their beliefs in the light of the disaster which had befallen them, and were helped to do so by two prophets.

The first was Ezekiel, a priest who prophesied both to the Jews in exile and to those remaining in the Holy Land. He condemned his people for their disloyalty to their covenant with God, and saw himself as a watchman warning against impending disaster. He stressed individual as well as communal responsibility. He preached judgment, but also looked forward to the restoration of Israel. In a vision he saw a valley of dry bones: the bones first became bodies and then had life breathed into them. The meaning of the vision was that through God's Spirit the Jewish people would be brought to life again, and restored to their own land.

The second prophet, whose teaching is recorded in the later chapters of the book of Isaiah, wrote from Babylon during the time when it began to decline. His message was one of hope and encouragement. He looked forward to the empire's overthrow by the Persians and to the return of the exiles to their own land. Several passages in his writing refer to a servant who would be led like a lamb to the slaughter: who would suffer on behalf of others, and by his suffering redeem them.

In 539 BC Babylon fell to the Persians, whose policy it was to send exiles back to their own lands and to encourage local customs of worship. In ensuing years groups of Jews returned to the area of the southern Kingdom and began the rebuilding of the Temple in Jerusalem, a work completed in 515 BC. The prophets Haggai and Zechariah encouraged the people in this achievement. Zechariah was one of several prophets who expected a Messiah who would reign over a purified Israel, which would be a light to the whole world.

Two great leaders, Ezra and Nehemiah, were sent by the Persian government to set the Jewish community in order. Ezra, a priest, re-imposed the Jewish law; Nehemiah, a secular leader, rebuilt the walls of Jerusalem and tried to improve the lot of the poor. Both leaders tried to re-create a God-centred nation and to prevent mixed marriages; the effect of their work was to divide the Jewish community in the south from the other peoples in the promised land.

Ezekiel; Isaiah 40 - 55; Haggai; Zechariah; Ezra; Nehemiah

Finding hope in desperate times

The years the Jews spent in exile in Babylon were times of great sadness and theological bewilderment. Why had their own omnipotent God of the whole earth allowed this to happen? Their reflections on this tragedy produced some of the most beautiful, and profound, poetry in the Bible. It is beautiful because of the images and words used. But, more importantly, it is beautiful because of the insights it offers.

'He was despised and rejected by men; a man of sorrows and acquainted with grief........surely he has borne our griefs and carried our sorrows'

Those words from Isaiah 53 develop the idea of a few people or even one person suffering on behalf of many. The following passage, from our own times, captures something similar:

'Who has inflicted this upon us? Who has made us Jews different from all other people? Who has allowed us to suffer so terribly up till now? It is God that has made us as we are, but it will be God, too, who will raise us up again. Who knows, it might even be our religion from which the world and all people will learn good, and for that reason and that reason only, do we have to suffer now'

Those are the words of Anne Frank, who died in the Nazi concentration camp at Belsen, aged 16. It is often through suffering, especially innocent suffering, that transformation comes and truth and love are made clear. The prophecies too which came out of the exile of the Jews dwelt on this theme – the suffering of the few for the sake of the whole. Christians believe that the same theme is continued in the life and death of Jesus.

Meditation

Growth out of disaster, life out of death is a recurring Biblical theme. How do people find hope in desperate situations? How do I cope when I am faced with overwhelming circumstances?

16 The Writings: Job and Ecclesiastes

The pre-Christian books of the Bible fall into four groups - the Pentateuch (the first five books), the Former and Latter Prophets (the books dealing with history and prophecy), and the Writings. Among the Writings are Psalms and Proverbs, the Song of Solomon (a book of love poems), Job and Ecclesiastes.

The book of Job explores the huge issue of undeserved suffering. It tells of a wealthy man blessed with a large family, who lived a virtuous and godly life. In conversation with one of his servants, Satan, God spoke well of Job. Satan, whose responsibility it was to act as the accuser of humankind, replied that Job's virtue was simply due to his prosperity. God therefore gave him permission to harass Job, though without harming him personally. So Satan deprived Job of his wealth and of his children; but Job, though grieving, accepted his fate, and said: 'The Lord gives and the Lord takes away; blessed be the name of the Lord'.

Then God gave Satan permission to afflict Job physically. He contracted sores from head to foot, and sat among ashes scraping himself with a shard of pottery. When three friends came to visit him, Job burst out in a terrible lament. One after another his friends tried to explain his affliction. Their main argument was that in some way he must have deserved it; but Job vehemently denied that this was so. Eventually however God revealed himself to Job in person, in all his creative splendour. Job exclaimed: 'I knew of you only by report, but now I see you with my own eyes', and submitted to him. God rewarded him by restoring his wealth and giving him a new family.

The book of Ecclesiastes was written by a teacher of wisdom reflecting in a spirit of free enquiry on the problems which life presents. Its message is that life is basically futile, since in the long run nothing changes: 'Vanity of vanities, all is vanity'. Even reflection is empty: 'In much wisdom is much vexation; the more knowledge, the more suffering'. One should make the best of this life, since it is all one has. There is a right time for everything, but no way of understanding God's purposes as a whole. Nonetheless, one should 'Fear God and obey his commandments'.

Job; Ecclesiastes

It isn't fair

Life is not straightforward, and it is good that holy scripture acknowledges this in the collection of 'the wisdom literature', of which Job and Ecclesiastes are two examples. This literature stands alongside the 'the law' of Moses and 'the word of God' as announced by the prophets. It comes out of reflection on the human experience of life and the insights and questions cross international and religious boundaries.

The book of Job has been called 'the Shakespeare of the Bible', because it deals with profound questions and offers the chance to reflect on them in the course of a moving drama. The book asks, 'Why does the good man Job suffer such colossal misfortune?' His friends argue with him about the matter but Job will not allow their suggestion that sin can account for calamity on this scale. The story gets so painful and almost unacceptable because it appears so disrespectful to God, who seems to be disinterested, even cruel. When, in the end, God puts Job in his place, Job acknowledges God's majesty. So the issue remains unresolved while acknowledging that God is in charge and everything is subject to him.

The book Ecclesiastes also contains realistic reflections on life. Often, the writer is something of a sceptic. For him, time is pitiless. He would agree with the Isaac Watts' hymn,

> 'Time, like an ever-rolling stream bears all its sons away;
>
> they fly, forgotten, as a dream dies at the opening day.'

But Ecclesiastes also says that time offers opportunities. When we look for the right moment, when the time is right, activity can be exhilarating and fruitful. Seizing the moment is a mark of an alert and sensitive life.

Meditation

Innocent suffering, like Job's, is a fact of life whether on a global scale or within the experience of ourselves and our friends. The question is not whether we can explain it in terms of fairness, which we can't, but how we come to terms with it.

Prayer

Lord God, if I am called upon to suffer, give me faith in your power to heal me and uphold me. Give me strength to do what is right when I encounter undeserved suffering.　　*Amen*

17 The centuries before the coming of Jesus

Many years after the event, stories were told of the heroism of the exiles living in Babylon during the period of captivity there. One story was about Shadrach, Meshach and Abednego, who were thrown into a burning fiery furnace because of their refusal to worship an idol set up by King Nebuchadnezzar. Assisted by an angel, they survived without harm, and from then on the King protected them in their religious practices.

Another story concerned a Jewish exile called Daniel. While King Belshazzar was giving a great feast, writing mysteriously appeared on the wall of his palace. None of the King's magicians were able to interpret the writing, but Daniel correctly told him that it pronounced doom upon his kingdom because of his idolatry.

In a third story King Darius the Mede, who by then had captured Babylon, was persuaded by some of his courtiers to issue an edict that no-one was to pray to anyone save himself. Daniel, now a leading royal servant, continued his practice of daily public prayer to the true God, and was condemned to be thrown into a den of lions. His faith ensured that he survived unharmed, and the enemies who had plotted his death were subjected to the fate they had intended for him.

A series of visions were granted to Daniel; between them they revealed the destiny of his people. The visions related to the rise and fall of successive empires culminating in the conquest of Persia by Alexander the Great. After Alexander's death in 323 BC. there was a long period of instability, during which there were attempts to stamp out traditional Jewish practices. The stories about Daniel and the visions attributed to him were an inspiration to those Jews determined to remain true to their faith.

Some versions of the Bible say nothing about the period between Alexander's conquests and the reign of Herod the Great, King of Judea, which began in 37 BC. Others include the Apocrypha, a collection of books dealing with those years. It was a time of constant warfare. When Herod the Great came to the throne it was as a nominee of the Romans, who were by then the dominant power in the whole Mediterranean area. It was also a time during which there was increasing expectation that a Messiah would come.

Daniel

The end of the beginning

We are now rapidly approaching the end of that part of the Bible written in Hebrew. The Jewish people had been back in their homeland for a couple of centuries, and the liberal Persian empire was leaving them alone. But then Alexander the Great conquered Persia, and Greek culture began to impinge on Judaism. Some, at least, of this was distasteful to conservative Jews. We can gain some 'feel' for this when we hear of the cultural and religious clashes around the world today. The result for the Jews at that time was tension which led, eventually, to outright wars.

The Book of Daniel dates from this war-torn period and looks at history between about 600BC and 164BC. Although not the last book in the Hebrew Scriptures, it was the last part of it to be written. It is Jewish propaganda addressed to Jews under pressure, designed to strengthen their resolve and loyalty to their own religious customs.

The parts of the Bible we have covered up till now have told the story of Israel's life and faith. It is a story which cannot be fully understood without the understanding that the Jews believed that God chose their people as the vehicle of his grace and fulfilment of his purposes. Their religious sense and faithfulness continue to this day. Out of that belief grew the Christian faith that Jesus is the fulfilment of God's promises to the Jews.

Meditation

The Hebrew Scriptures, of which we now have an overview, present a growing understanding of the nature of God. This understanding came through ancient tales passed from one generation to another, personal stories of great figures, tribal and national histories, sublime poetry with deep spiritual insight and the faith and vision of men and women who themselves were close to God. The true nature of God was also perceived through his dealings with fallible people and often with rogues. How has our understanding of God grown as we have been reading these pages?

Prayer

O God, may understanding of yourself and your ways grow within me.   Amen

18 The visions of Zechariah and Mary

During the reign of Herod the Great a priest called Zechariah had a vision while he was on duty in the temple in Jerusalem. An angel told him that he and his wife Elizabeth would have a son who was to be called John, meaning 'The Lord is gracious'. This would happen even though they were both past the normal age of childbearing. Zechariah doubted this divine message; in consequence he lost the power of speech.

Soon afterwards Elizabeth conceived. When she was six months pregnant a young relation of hers, called Mary, was visited by an angel, who told her that she too had been chosen by God to give birth to a son. He would be called the Son of God, and would become a king of David's line for ever. Mary exclaimed: 'How can this happen? I am still a virgin'. The angel replied 'The conception will be the work of the Holy Spirit'. Mary accepted the angel's message, and went to share her good news with Elizabeth. Elizabeth blessed Mary for her faith and told her that when she arrived she felt her own child leap within her.

Mary rejoiced with these words:

> 'My soul praises God and my spirit rejoices in God my Saviour, because he has chosen a lowly young woman to be the instrument of his saving power.
>
> From now on, everyone shall call me blessed; for the holy and mighty God has done great things for me.
>
> God has shown his mercy upon succeeding generations; upon all who fear him.
>
> In his strength he has defeated the proud and their schemes, humbling the powerful and exalting the humble; feeding the hungry and sending the rich away empty.
>
> He has fulfilled his ancient promises to the people of Israel, and he has shown mercy to Abraham's children for ever.'

When Elizabeth's baby was born, after Mary had returned to her home, local people expected he would be called Zechariah after his father. However, because of God's message to her husband, Elizabeth insisted that he should be called John. When they asked Zechariah what he thought, he took a writing-tablet and supported his wife. Immediately he was able to speak again, and prophesied that his son would be the forerunner of someone even greater.

Luke 1

God's promises are fulfilled

The Jewish story, which we have seen developing in the preceding pages, now takes a major leap forward. The events which will now be described led some Jews to leave their mainstream tradition. They gave birth to a new sect – initially within Judaism – which became what we now call Christianity. Christ himself was a both a fulfilment of the Jewish understanding of God and also a completely new and radical revelation of God's nature.

The scriptures from this point on, this 'new testament' or 'new covenant' are the basis of Christianity and consist of four accounts of the life of Jesus (the text opposite is based on just one of them, Luke's); an account of the first Christian church's activities; many letters, mostly by Paul; and a vision of the end of time.

This new writing for a new era opens with strange events. No doubt at the time they were perceived as miraculous: an old couple and a virgin suddenly each expect a child. The first is perhaps not so impossible. But what we know about conception makes the second one harder for many to believe possible. However, for people at the time and in the traditions of the church down the ages, each event has powerfully signalled that God was at work.

On each occasion the recipients of the good news celebrate with a poem – Zechariah's and Mary's songs. Part of Mary's is given opposite. Each looks back to prophecies in the Jewish scriptures and roots both events there, in God's ancient promises to Abraham and David. Each, but especially Mary's, has been seen to be culturally revolutionary with its references to God favouring the lowly and humble over the rich and proud.

John, the older child, grew up to be a turbulent character and became a vastly popular, if ascetic, preacher, who attracted immense crowds. We shall come across him again in section 21.

Meditation

The miraculous nature of Christ's coming into the world seeks to account for the inexplicable in Christ's character and life. Should it surprise us that an event as cosmic as the coming of God in human form takes place in ways which are different from the natural order of things?

Mary was engaged to a carpenter called Joseph, who lived in the town of Nazareth in the northern province of Galilee, and who was a just and upright man. When he discovered she was pregnant his first intention was to separate from her. Then an angel appeared to him in a dream, told him of the child's divine origin, and commanded him to call him 'Jesus', which means 'God saves'. Joseph was obedient to this vision. He took Mary as his wife, but they did not consummate their marriage until her son was born.

At that time the Roman Emperor Augustus ordered a census. Because he was a descendant of King David, Joseph returned to David's native city of Bethlehem to register, taking the pregnant Mary with him. Jesus was born in Bethlehem, in a stable because the inn was full.

An angel appeared to a group of shepherds grazing their flocks nearby. They were terrified, but the angel told them that he came with good news. The Christ (that is, the anointed King) had been born in Bethlehem; they would find him wrapped in strips of cloth and lying in a manger. Then a great host of angels appeared, praising God and promising peace to those he favoured. The shepherds went to Bethlehem, visited the family, and spread the news that this was a very special baby. After eight days he was circumcised and the name Jesus formally conferred upon him.

A few weeks later his parents took Jesus to the Temple in Jerusalem to perform the rites associated with the birth of a first-born son. While they were there two holy people – a man called Simeon and an elderly woman called Anna – blessed Jesus and foresaw a great destiny for him. Simeon prayed:

'Lord, now permit your servant to die in peace, according to your promise.

For I have seen the salvation which you have prepared before all the nations, to serve as a revelation to those who are not Jews, and to glorify your own people Israel'.

Simeon warned Mary that suffering lay ahead, for her son and for herself, while Anna talked about him to everyone hoping for the deliverance of the people of Israel.

Matthew 1.18-25; Luke 2.1-38

The event around which Christian history turns

The drama of the Christmas story, so well known to us, mixes many of the ingredients of a fascinating tale - scandal, mystical dreams, good but poor people, their baby born in a stable, then angels and kings.

To those who first told and recorded the story, each ingredient had an important symbolic significance. Together they say that this was no normal birth. Its significance was summed up when Joseph and Mary, following the usual customs, obeyed the old Law and took their little baby for his first visit to the Temple in nearby Jerusalem.

Because Jews remember with gratitude their escape from calamity in Egypt[1], each of their own first-born boys is 'given' to God – only to be 'bought back'. It was this ceremony that brought Joseph and Mary, with their baby, to the Temple. There, as the text opposite recounts, two faithful people recognised that this baby was special.

There is potential for every new-born child to do or be something special. Simeon's poem, now known as the Nunc Dimittis, celebrates his prophetic insight that this child was to become a great leader – not just of his own Jewish people, but internationally – but that this would not be without suffering. Anna, who lived in the Temple had a similar prophetic vision.

The deepest significance of all these events, however, only dawned on Christians later. John, Jesus' disciple (not the son of Elizabeth) describes the coming of Jesus like a new creation of the world. Just as the Genesis story of creation describes God, by His word, bringing light into the world, so the coming of Jesus was brought about by the power of God bringing new light and hope to the world.[2]

Meditation

Am I alert to spot how God, present in everyone, makes all people special, unique and worthy of reverence and compassion?

Prayer

Put me, Lord, in the way of your light that I may have the faith to recognise Jesus as your new creation.   Amen

[1] Section 4   [2] John 1.1-14

20 Jesus' early life

While the holy family were still living in Bethlehem wise men from the east came in search of a newly born king of the Jews. They were guided by a star, but they also sought help from King Herod. He was alarmed by their mission, but, after consultation with religious leaders, he directed them to Bethlehem where the prophet Micah had foretold a king would be born. He enquired when the star guiding them had appeared, and asked them to return to him when they had found the child, so that he too could pay homage to him. The wise men followed the star to Bethlehem, visited the holy family, worshipped the child, and presented him with gifts of gold, incense and myrrh.

Suspecting Herod's intentions, the wise men returned home another way, while Joseph was warned in a dream to take his wife and child to safety in Egypt. It was as well he did so, since Herod, in fear for his throne, ordered a massacre of all boys under the age of two in the Bethlehem region. It was not until Herod died that Joseph was able to take his family back to his own country, to live in Nazareth.

When Jesus reached the age of twelve he went with his family and friends to Jerusalem for the annual feast of the Passover. On the journey home his family did not miss him until they had gone some distance. Immediately they returned to Jerusalem and spent three days searching for him. At last they found him in the Temple, engaged in discussion with the teachers there, and astonishing them with his intelligence. His mother asked: 'Why have you treated us like this? Your father and I have been looking for you anxiously.' Jesus replied: 'Did you not realise I would be in my Father's house?' Then he went back to Nazareth with them, remained an obedient son in the family home, and followed the trade of a carpenter until he was about thirty years old.

Matthew 2; Mark 6.3; Luke 2.41-52, 3.23

Childlike or childish?

The accounts of the birth of Jesus continue with the visit of 'the three wise men'. The Bible actually says they were astrologers, probably from Persia (Iran, today). So they were foreigners and probably not Jews. They brought expensive gifts with them because the stars had told them that the child they would find was indeed a king. This was political dynamite in a land under Roman domination, where there was a steady undercurrent of incipient rebellion and where King Herod was an unpopular puppet of the Romans. The upshot was, the family became refugees in Egypt.

When eventually Mary, Joseph and Jesus were able to return, it was to their home in rural Nazareth[1]. Jesus grew up there and learnt a trade in a very ordinary family.

However, there was an upset when the family returned south to Jerusalem to celebrate the Passover. As a 12-year old, Jesus was now, ritually, an adult, whose duty it was to make this pilgrimage at least once in his life. The Jerusalem Temple was not just a place of worship: it was a place of scholarly learning and discussion. Here this provincial lad would find sophistication and encounter intellectual depth. His imagination was evidently captured by the thrill of it all: arguing about his Jewish heritage with some of the greatest teachers of his day. Lost in admiration and excitement he also lost touch with his parents! Childlike curiosity served him well. It was the beginning of an adventure of his mind and spirit.

It was clearly during the next eighteen or so years that Jesus had a growing understanding of his own significance and destiny. This was to come to full realisation at his baptism

Meditation

That attractive, open and curious mind of a child is something we should treasure. It is probably why Jesus treated children with such importance. We can be childlike too. Childishness, which fails to bring our maturity to bear on our faith, is best left to childhood. An adult life needs an adult faith. What events in our own childhood have had a profound effect on us? As we have grown physically and intellectually, have we grown spiritually as well?

[1] See map on page 55

21 Jesus' baptism and temptations

John, son of Zechariah and Elizabeth, chose to live an austere life in the Judean desert. He wore a garment of camel's hair and lived on locusts and wild honey. He preached a demanding message in which he offered baptism with water as a sign of repentance and the forgiveness of sins. Huge crowds came to hear him, and were baptised in the River Jordan. When Jewish spiritual leaders joined those coming to be baptised, John told them not to rely on their Israelite heritage for salvation, but to lead better lives. He prophesied that there was someone far greater than himself coming after him, whose sandals he was unworthy to remove. This greater one would baptise, not with water, but with the life of God, the Holy Spirit.

Jesus was among those who offered themselves for baptism. At first John tried to dissuade him, saying: 'It is I who need to be baptised by you'. Eventually however Jesus persuaded him to perform the ceremony by saying: 'We should do everything which God requires'. So John baptised Jesus; as he came up from the water the Holy Spirit descended upon him in the form of a dove, and a voice from heaven declared: 'This is my son, the Beloved, with whom I am well pleased'.

Then the Holy Spirit led Jesus into the desert, where he spent forty days fasting and praying. During that time the devil appeared to him and tried to persuade him to misuse the special powers which God had given him; but he resisted successfully, relying on the guidance of the Scriptures, the sacred writings of the Jewish faith. Tempted in his hunger to turn stones into bread, he replied: 'Man does not live only by bread, but by the word of God'. Tempted to throw himself down from the parapet of the Temple in Jerusalem, relying on angels to protect him, he replied: 'Scripture says you should not put God to the test'. Tempted to become an earthly king at the price of doing the devil homage he replied: 'You shall worship God alone'. Then the devil left him, and angels came and ministered to him.

Soon after he had baptised Jesus, John was arrested and thrown into prison for criticising Herod, ruler of the province of Galilee and son of Herod the Great, for marrying his close relation Herodias.

Matthew 3, 4; Mark 1.14, 6.17-18

Jesus finds his priorities

Two men dominate this section. John and Jesus.

John was the last of the great Jewish prophets. His style reflects scenes from the life of Elijah (see section 11). He was an ascetic who lived in the wilderness, but who drew vast crowds to hear his stark, demanding words. In his day, John was possibly more famous than Jesus and so Jesus probably came to listen to him along with everyone else. As we have seen in the previous section Jesus was serious about his religion.

John used to baptise people in water as a sign they wanted to change their life-styles. Jesus asked John to baptise him. Why? Jesus was already sincere and serious about his faith. But he wanted to be true to his Jewish roots – 'what God requires' - and to identify himself with the call to repentance which John was preaching.

It is quite possible that it was at that moment Jesus perceived his vocation. Standing in the water of the old river Jordan, Jesus heard a voice. The text opposite quotes Matthew's account: compare it with Mark's: 'You are my son, my beloved.'

The temptations of Jesus and His response are a clear indication of the priorities and direction of His ministry. He was neither to overwhelm people by His miraculous powers nor to introduce a new kingdom by military force or political guile. He believed he had come to fulfil the Hebrew Scriptures and introduce not a nation in the political sense but a spiritual kingdom which required a whole new way of living.

Meditation

So what do you think of him so far? From the beginning of his public appearances Jesus caused a stir. For some he was a curiosity, just one of many preachers of his day. For others he was suspected of usurping the sacred traditions of Jewish teaching. Some were astonished at his miracles. If we had been in the crowd what would we have begun to think?

Prayer

Lord God, help me to see the real Jesus and give me the faith to call him friend.   Amen

22 Jesus begins his ministry

After John's arrest Jesus began his active ministry. His message was: 'The time has come; the rule of God is close at hand; repent and believe the good news'.

For his first disciples Jesus called from their nets two pairs of fishermen - Simon (whom he nicknamed Peter - 'the Rock') and Andrew, sons of Jonah; and James and John, sons of Zebedee. He soon became well known and much talked about. People from a wide area came to hear his teaching and to be healed of sickness. However when he brought his message to his home town of Nazareth he ran into trouble. In an address in the synagogue (the local place of worship) he quoted words of the prophet Isaiah:

'The Spirit of the Lord is upon me because he has anointed me; he has sent me to announce good news to the poor, to proclaim release for prisoners and recovery of sight for the blind; to proclaim the year of the Lord's favour.'

He then told his hearers that this prophecy was being fulfilled that very day. Remembering his humble background, they were astonished at his implied claim that he was, at the least, a prophet. When Jesus rebuked them for their lack of faith, they reacted with such hostility that he barely escaped with his life.

From his prison John heard about the progress of Jesus' ministry. He sent two of his followers to ask Jesus: 'Are you the One we are expecting, or is he still to come?' Jesus replied indirectly, by pointing to his healing work and to the good news he was bringing to the poor, and by saying: 'Happy is he who has no doubts about me'.

Herod stood in awe of John, and liked to listen to his teaching. His wife Herodias however hated him because of his opposition to her marriage. During Herod's birthday celebrations, a dance by Herodias' daughter so delighted him that he offered her anything she wanted. At her mother's instigation she asked for the head of John on a plate. Reluctantly, Herod ordered his execution. John's head was given to the girl, and she gave it to her mother.

Mark 1.14-45, 6.14-29; Luke 3.23, 4.16-30, 7.18-23

A public manifesto

Jesus was a country lad. It is well to remember his humble, simple background. His home town was Nazareth, a small settlement in the provinces and far from the action and sophistication of the capital, Jerusalem.

It was in Nazareth and the nearby towns that he first tried out his preaching. We are told that he set out his manifesto in words from Isaiah: he is to address marginalised people, like himself, with good news. We might have expected that people from his home town would have been glad that a prominent preacher, perhaps even the long promised Messiah, was to be from amongst them. But, as so often happens, 'familiarity breeds contempt'. Perhaps his contemporaries were envious. The refusal of some to welcome good news will certainly be a repeated theme throughout Jesus' life and it has also been evident throughout history.

As we have seen, John, the man who had baptised Jesus and started him off, was perhaps more inclined to be positive. But by this time he was in prison and even he wanted reassurance but Jesus would not give a direct 'yes' or 'no' reply. This was typical of his style: was it because people had to learn to trust their own instincts about him? He could not do it for them. We shall return to this theme.[1]

Meditation

Where, at the end of the day, do we put our trust? What is 'bed rock' for us? How shall we decide what is worth following? And what do we have to grow out of?

Prayer

Lord God, I am conscious of faltering and wavering in my search for you. Thank you for searching me out so patiently. Be the rock around which I build my life.   Amen

[1] See section 27

23 Jesus' ministry continues

Initially Jesus ministered in his home province of Galilee, in the north of the promised land. In the synagogue in the town of Capernaum he astonished his fellow-worshippers one Sabbath, by teaching on his own authority rather than by relying exclusively on the Scriptures, and by healing a man possessed by a demon. That same day he performed other miracles of healing, and in the days which followed many more. He cured a man of leprosy simply by touching him.

He tried to avoid publicity for his miracles, but nonetheless crowds gathered wherever he went. A group carrying a paralysed man went so far as to break open a roof in order to lower him to Jesus' feet for healing. On another occasion, to escape the crush, he taught from a boat while the people stood on the shore.

Jesus soon became involved in controversy. He gave offence by forgiving sins, a power which most Jews thought was reserved to God alone. He also mixed freely with social outcasts, such as the men who collected taxes on behalf of the Romans, saying that he came to call sinners, not the righteous. On occasions when others fasted, he and his disciples did not do so. He said: 'A bridegroom's friends do not fast while the bridegroom is with them. While the bridegroom is present, it is right to feast; the time for fasting will come when the bridegroom has been taken away'.

Jesus gave priority to human need over the detailed demands of the Jewish Law. He said: 'The Sabbath was made for man, not man for the Sabbath: the Son of Man (by whom he meant himself) is Lord even of the Sabbath'. Accepting a direct challenge from his critics, he healed a man with a withered arm in a synagogue on the Sabbath day. His opponents accused him of being possessed by an evil spirit; to which he retorted: 'If I am driving evil spirits out of people by means of an evil spirit then the reign of evil is about to collapse.'

Mark 1–3

Clashes with the authorities

In the previous two sections there is no doubt Jesus saw himself as having a special calling from God. This gave him a sense of his own special authority. Of course not everyone recognised that authority and many felt threatened by it.

Jesus had many reasons for taking the stand he did. From the time when, as a boy, he had discussed with the teachers of the law in the temple in Jerusalem (see section 20) we can be sure he steeped himself in the scriptures of his people. And it wasn't just knowledge he gained there: it was also insight – insight brought about by his own closeness to God. He perceived more deeply than many senior to himself the inner meaning of the scriptures, and how they communicated the loving desire of God for his people's welfare – that is, their growth towards their God. Hence he felt confident, on occasion, to challenge the 'official' line, as he did in Capernaum, described in the first paragraph opposite.

He deeply understood the purpose of the Law which God had handed down through Moses. It was to keep God in peoples' hearts and minds. He also understood that the vast amount of traditional interpretation which had come to surround the Law was only man-made, and where it inhibited people from understanding its true meaning it had to be challenged and, if necessary, rejected. This made him an enemy of many religious leaders whose authority over the people rested on their interpretations of traditions contained in the Law.

Meditation

For the Jews of Jesus's time, the Law was what held their race together and it gave a constant reminder of God being amongst them. The insight Jesus brought was that concentrating on the detailed traditions prevented people from seeing the wider vision – the underlying purpose of their call as God's people. Can we distinguish between the tradition of faith which keeps God before us and our traditions about which we can be too defensive?

Provinces at the time of Jesus

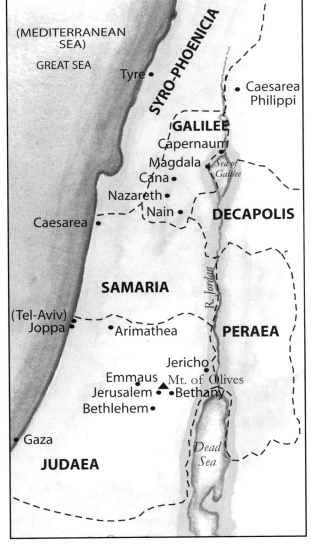

Historic Names
(Modern Names)
PROVINCES

40 Miles
40 Kms

(MEDITERRANEAN
SEA)

GREAT SEA

SYRO-PHOENICIA

Tyre •

• Caesarea
Philippi

GALILEE

Capernaum •

Magdala • Sea of Galilee

Cana •

Nazareth •

Nain •

DECAPOLIS

Caesarea •

R. Jordan

SAMARIA

(Tel-Aviv)
Joppa •

• Arimathea

PERAEA

Jericho

Emmaus   Mt. of Olives
Jerusalem • • Bethany
Bethlehem •

• Gaza

Dead
Sea

JUDAEA

24 Jesus chooses the Twelve

After spending a night in prayer, Jesus picked out from his followers twelve men whom he named apostles, a word meaning 'those who are sent'. They included the two pairs of brothers already mentioned - Peter and Andrew, and James and John; Jesus nicknamed the latter 'sons of thunder'. Matthew, whom Jesus had also called from his work to follow him, was a tax-gatherer, a member of a despised profession. Other apostles were Philip, Bartholomew, Thomas the twin, James son of Alphaeus, Judas son of James, and Simon, who had been a member of the Jewish armed resistance. Finally there was Judas Iscariot, who was later to betray him. Jesus was also attended by a group of women, some of whom he had healed, who cared for him and for the Twelve out of their own resources. They included Mary from the town of Magdala and Joanna, wife of King Herod's steward. Other followers, in larger or smaller numbers, came and went from time to time.

Jesus made it very clear that loyalty to himself overrode all other loyalties. For example, when members of his family, fearing that he was out of his mind, came to take him home he refused to go to them, saying: 'Whoever does the will of God is my brother and sister and mother.'

In due course Jesus sent the Twelve out two by two to preach and heal as he was doing. He told them to take nothing except a staff for the journey - no food, no wallet, no money and no change of clothing. They were to rely on the hospitality of others to meet their needs.

Later still Jesus sent out seventy-two of his followers on a similar mission and with the same instructions. He told them that whoever listened to them listened to him, and whoever rejected them rejected him. The seventy-two returned rejoicing in their success. Jesus rejoiced with them, and thanked his Father in heaven who had revealed to common people what was hidden from the learned. He added: 'Everything is entrusted to me by my Father. Only the Father knows who the Son is, and only the Son and those whom the Son instructs truly know the Father.'

Matthew 9.9; Mark 3.17, 31-35, 6.7-13; Luke 6.12-16, 8.1-3, 10.1-24

The Twelve are shaped by Jesus

Why twelve? It's another example of Jesus deliberately rooting himself in the history, tradition and culture of his people, the Jewish people.

From the time of Abraham and his son Isaac, the Jews had been gathered into twelve tribes – named after the children of Jacob. As we have seen, their coming together as a single nation came later.[1] By choosing 12 disciples to follow him and develop his own ministry Jesus is saying, in effect, that he is setting up a renewed Israel.

The Twelve were a mixed bunch. They weren't always very quick-witted and sometimes totally missed the point of what Jesus told them. Peter emerges as a leading light, though his impetuosity got him into trouble. John seems to have been the one closest to Jesus. They were all loyal except Judas, who informed on Jesus and then committed suicide. The rest stuck with Jesus – until the moment of his arrest. Then they all fled from the fearful scene; but soon came together again.

At the point of their call, however, they were keen to listen to Jesus and to follow his teaching and training. They were men ready to live simply and to carry the news of Jesus and his teaching around the villages and countryside. But they were very much learners and their weaknesses are as evident as their strengths. This set a pattern for Jesus's followers for all time. Their priority is not their own comfort, they know they have much to learn, they have a passion to point people to Jesus and they are frequently surprised by what God achieves through them.

Meditation

One of the wonderful things about the disciples, and much of the church ever since, is that huge responsibility is given to ordinary, fallible people. Do we make an excuse of our 'ordinariness' not to become involved amongst the followers of Jesus?

Prayer

Make your way for my life plain to me, O God.   *Amen*

[1] Section 7

25 The Sermon on the Mount

Much of Jesus' teaching was brought together when, seated on a hillside, he spoke to his disciples about life in the kingdom of God. He taught that true happiness comes from having the right attitudes. Those who are humble, concerned about the world's sinfulness, gentle, devoted to goodness, merciful, single-minded in God's service, and peace-lovers will be blessed by God. Those of his followers who are persecuted in this world should rejoice, because they will have a rich reward in the next.

Jesus emphasised that he had not come to destroy the moral demands of the Jewish Law but to fulfil them. He taught that it is not enough not to commit murder; the anger which can lead to murder must be set aside too. It is not enough not to commit adultery; lustful thoughts must be set aside too. It is not enough to keep only our solemn promises; we should always mean what we say.

The Jewish Law taught that retaliation should be proportionate to the harm done - an eye for an eye and a tooth for a tooth - but Jesus taught that we should love our enemies and that we should return good for evil, turning the other cheek when others attack us.

He went on to say that ostentatious piety and charitable giving are wrong; both piety and giving should be between ourselves and God. No-one can serve two masters; it is impossible to serve both God and money. God knows what people's needs are and will supply them, in the same way as he provides food for birds and glorious clothing for flowers; we should not be anxious but should trust him. We should not judge others; for we shall be judged to the degree we judge. It is difficult to find the way to the kingdom of heaven and there will be those who will try to mislead us. We should assess others by the moral and spiritual quality of their lives.

He summarised the whole moral teaching of the Old Testament in the command to treat others as you would like them to treat you.

Jesus said that anyone who acts on his words is like a wise man who built his house on a rock. When storms came the house stood firm. But anyone who does not act on his words is like a man who built his house on sand. When storms came the house fell, and the ensuing devastation was great.

Matthew 5-7

An inner life style

The Sermon on the Mount is perhaps the most well known and profound teaching of Jesus. It is summarised opposite.

The teaching ranges over many subjects, but at its core are 'the beatitudes', a collection of memorable sayings. These are celebrated by Christians and non-Christians alike as a summary of a deeply spiritual understanding of life.

Those who follow this guidance are the happy and fortunate ones – even though, as the sayings make clear, this is not what we might initially expect. But in effect, each saying is expressing a truth about God himself: he is humble, merciful, eager for justice, eager for peace. So the sermon is not just about arbitrary values and ways of behaving, but more about how our lives are to reflect truths deep within God.

The Sermon on the Mount is not so much about being good as being godly – which is an altogether bigger vision. Seeing, hearing, understanding with the mind of God, and responding accordingly. The topic is not morality so much as holiness. Indeed, exclusive concern for moral 'purity' is one of the things Jesus attacks most fiercely.

What matters most, Jesus is saying, is the state of the heart and mind from which actions emerge. It is not just killing, stealing or committing adultery which is wrong but the attitudes and inner thoughts which lead to them. Leading a holy and godly life is much more than keeping on the right side of the law. It is more than not being found out; it is seeking to be what God made us for – to reflect his being within ourselves and through our lives. It is knowing that God understands everything within our hearts.

The closing sentences opposite are proved true over and over again. The foundations on which our lives are built condition every action and ultimately lead to our destiny. An unprincipled person will flounder; a hypocrite will be lost in self deceit. One who has faith and trusts God as the rock of their life will grasp the purpose of life, however many times they have to pick themselves from failure.

Meditation

In the Sermon on the Mount Jesus points to a radical new life style. Are we ready to face that kind of challenge?

26 Teaching on prayer

Both in the Sermon on the Mount and at other times Jesus taught about prayer. Personal prayer is a private matter and should not be paraded in front of others. Prayer offered in faith always receives an answer. 'Ask, and you will receive; seek, and you will find; knock, and the door will be opened to you.' There is no point in aimless repetition, since God knows what you need before you tell him; but perseverance in prayer is a virtue. Jesus drove this point home by telling a story about a widow who so pestered an unjust judge that finally, in exasperation, he gave her her due. If a man of that kind would behave in that way, is it likely that God will ignore those who cry out to him day and night?

Jesus taught his followers to pray in these words:

> 'Our Father in heaven, hallowed be your name.
> Your kingdom come and your will be done,
> on earth as it is in heaven.
>
> Give us this day our daily bread,
> and forgive us the wrong we have done,
> just as we have forgiven those who have wronged us.
>
> And do not bring us to the time of testing,
> but rescue us from the evil one.'

Jesus taught that effective prayer depends upon humility. He told a story about a Pharisee and a tax-gatherer praying in the Temple. The Pharisee prayed: 'I thank you, God, that I am not greedy, dishonest or adulterous as other people are, or like this tax-gatherer. I fast regularly and pay my religious taxes'. The tax-gatherer did not even dare look up, but beat his breast saying: 'God, have mercy on me, a sinner'. Of the two, it was the tax-gatherer who went home forgiven.

Jesus set a personal example of prayer. He frequently went away into seclusion for extended times of prayer. His cures were often accompanied by prayer, and he passed the evening of his final arrest largely in prayer. First, in the upper room, he prayed for his friends and followers; then, in the Garden of Gethsemane, he prayed for himself.

Matthew 6.5-13, 14.23; Luke 11.9, 18.1-14, 22.39-46; John 17

Listening and speaking to God

Jesus prayed a lot. This fact can be rather daunting, giving the feeling that 'Jesus was holy but I'm not up to it'. But it need not be like that. As the text opposite shows, Jesus spent extended times alone, praying whole nights, sometimes. Prayer like that isn't so much 'talking' as 'being' and 'listening': what our heart says when we put ourselves near God. When we do 'talk' to God, Jesus has given us words to use – as described opposite.

But notice those words speak of 'us' and 'our', rather than 'me' and 'mine'. And that reminds us of another central thing about Jesus' prayer. He prayed in company – and he prayed alone. He went, like every devout Jew, to the public prayers in the synagogue. Perhaps that's where he first learned to pray. He learned to pray privately by learning to pray communally. It's that way round for us, too. It is also no bad thing to have a 'soul friend' with whom we can, openly and in confidence, talk about how our own spiritual journey is going. Taken together, all this helps prevent our prayer becoming, on the one hand, self-indulgent like the Pharisee in Jesus' story, and, on the other, frightening when the demands it brings seem tough.

So before we attempt whole nights of solitary prayer, we can start more simply! Praying with others is always an encouragement, either in church or more intimately with friends. But Jesus tells there are times when we should 'go into our room, shut the door, and pray to our Father who sees in secret'[1]

Meditation

All of us are learners when it comes to prayer. Attentive listening can be difficult but silently absorbing the presence of God can be immensely valuable. When it comes to words, it is often the simplest prayers which are the best. We will be surprised how God honours our small sparks of faith.

Prayer

Lord, give me a listening ear and help me to find words to pray. Listen to my inner desires and longings, even when I cannot express them myself. Then, O God, surprise me.   Amen

[1] Matthew 6.6

27 Parables

Much of Jesus' teaching was in parables - memorable stories, drawn from people's everyday experience, which convey a spiritual meaning.

He spoke, for example, of a sower scattering seed widely over a field. Some fell on the footpath and was quickly eaten by birds. Some fell on rocky ground with little soil; it sprang up quickly but soon withered under the sun's rays. Some fell among thistles which choked it as it grew; and some fell on good ground and produced an abundant crop.

Jesus later explained to his disciples that the seed was the word of God. Some hear it and immediately forget it. Some receive it with enthusiasm, but have no staying power. Some receive it, but it is soon choked by worldly cares and pleasures; and some accept it and bear the fruit of lives pleasing to God.

To a lawyer who asked him who should count as a neighbour he responded with a parable about a man who was attacked on a lonely road by robbers who left him half-dead. When they saw the victim, both a priest and a Temple servant passed by on the other side of the road and did nothing to help him. But a Samaritan (a man from a community the Jews hated and despised) took pity on him. He tended his wounds, took him to an inn, and paid the innkeeper to take care of him. 'Which of the three', asked Jesus, 'was neighbour to the man who had been attacked?' The lawyer replied: 'The one who showed him kindness.' Jesus concluded: 'Go and do as he did.'

To illustrate the generous love of God Jesus told a story about a landowner who had two sons. One day the younger asked for his inheritance and then went away and wasted it on foolish and extravagant living. Having lost everything, he decided to return home and to throw himself on his father's mercy. When he was still a long way away his father saw him coming, ran to meet him, forgave him on the spot and arranged a huge party for him. However this infuriated the elder son, who had stayed at home and worked hard, never putting a foot wrong. He complained bitterly to his father about the fact that his brother was being treated more generously than himself. In reply his father reminded him that he was heir to the whole estate, but insisted that it was right to rejoice when a lost child came home.

Mark 4.1-20; Luke 10.25-37, 15.11-32

Finding the truth behind the story

Many teachers use stories to illustrate their points. Jesus certainly did. But his 'parables' also work at a deeper level. The truth he wanted to get across had to be received in his listeners' innermost hearts – not just in their heads. He was dealing in 'heart truth', not just 'head truths'. So he often came at things sideways on. He acted and spoke symbolically.

You can't really 'explain' his parables. Jesus rarely tried to. This seems baffling at first – especially if he's trying to get his message across. But another word for parable is riddle – or joke. If you explain a riddle, you lose the point. It you explain a joke, your listener may get it, but probably not laugh. They may even think you boring!

Jesus' stories often start with the familiar. In the examples opposite, people knew about seeds growing, about priests who had no compassion, about children who rebelled. Hearing such stories, people would relax, open up, and enter into them. It was all going on 'at a safe distance'. But often the story then took an unexpected turn. His listeners were caught unawares. If they had identified with the 'goodies' in the story, they might then find they weren't the goodies after all! The 'safe distance' had evaporated. And sometimes his parables got Jesus into trouble: when the authorities realised many of his parables were against them.

But those who 'got' the point never forgot it. The unexpected twist meant it had reached the heart, not just the head – for better or worse. And those who followed him then, did so because the penny had dropped. They now saw for themselves, not just because someone else (even Jesus) said so.

Meditation

Think of a time when you have been looking at a picture or heard a story which has at first baffled us. It may be some time later that the penny drops and we see what we didn't see before or catch the meaning of the story. Insight into the truth of God can often be like that. We need to treasure those moments of enlightenment and make them part of our personal development.

28 Jesus answers questions

During his ministry Jesus was often questioned: by his disciples, by those genuinely anxious to learn from him, and by those trying to catch him out. Asked by some strict Jews why his disciples did not observe the laws relating to ritual cleanliness, such as the symbolic washing of hands before a meal, he replied that it was easy to concentrate on such matters and to ignore the demands of the moral law. As regards dietary restrictions, he taught that it was not what people took in that harmed them but what came out of them - the evil thoughts, words and deeds which come from the human heart.

Jesus was also asked about divorce. He replied that the permission to divorce given in the law of Moses had been a concession to human weakness. God's will is that a man and his wife should no longer be two persons but one. Human beings should not divide those whom God has joined. Anyone who divorces and remarries commits adultery.

To a rich man who asked what he should do to obtain eternal life, Jesus replied that he should keep the moral commandments given through Moses. Assured by the man that he already did so, Jesus advised him to sell everything he had, to give the proceeds to the poor, and to follow him. The man went away sadly. Jesus reflected that it was easier for a camel to pass through the eye of a needle than for a wealthy person to enter the kingdom of God. However, those who leave everything to follow him will be richly rewarded, in this world and the next.

His disciples asked him: 'Who is greatest in the kingdom of heaven?' Jesus set a child in front of them, and said: 'Unless you become as humble as a child you will never enter the kingdom of heaven. Those who are like children will be greatest in the kingdom of heaven, and whoever receives a child in my name receives me.'

Peter asked Jesus: 'how many times should I forgive someone who has sinned against me? Seven times?' 'No,' said Jesus: 'seventy times seven.' To expand the point he told a story about a king who forgave one of his servants a fortune, only to discover that the servant immediately demanded the repayment of a much smaller debt from a fellow-servant. The king punished the unforgiving servant; similarly, God will punish us for our offences against him unless we forgive others for their offences against us.

Mark 7.1-23, 10.1-31; Matthew 18.1-5, 21-35

The letter of the law and the way of love

Jesus's claim was that he had come to fulfil the Law of Moses. The questions he faced were put to him by serious-minded followers of the Law, people such as the Scribes and Pharisees. These religious leaders had devoted their lives to holy living under the Law, but over time the original Law of Moses had become more obscure by a host of minute rules and regulations. They were genuinely curious about what this new teacher would say about the ethical issues of the day.

Jesus stressed the relationship of love and trust between God and his people, which was one strand of the Jewish tradition and he wanted to release people from the burdensome regulations of the Law. He longed to show that there is a new way of grace based on a love of humanity and forgiveness for failings. So what you eat, or how you behave towards your spouse, or what you do with your money is not about following regulations but really about responding to God's love and forgiveness for us all.

Jesus demonstrated this with a visual aid: he took a child and spoke of how the simplicity and the smallness of childhood demonstrate God's way with us all. God is neither legalistic nor is he abusive in his use of power, but He meets us in the little things and in humility and loving service to one another.

Meditation

Where do we find guidance to help us with the big questions of life? Do we think that God is powerful and can answer them for us, or do we look to God in prayerful attention, asking that we may cooperate with him in love and forgiveness?

Prayer

O God, we ask that we may serve you in simplicity and in faith and that you will guide us into the new way of grace which Jesus came to bring to us and to all mankind.   Amen

29 Miracles of healing

During his travels Jesus was sometimes asked to perform miracles in order to demonstrate his powers; but he always refused, performing miracles only in response to real need. He tried to avoid them becoming general knowledge, but they often did so, filling those who saw or heard about them with amazement and awe.

On one occasion he was confronted by a man possessed by demons, who had proved uncontrollable and who lived in a graveyard. As was often the case, the demons recognised Jesus for whom he was, calling him 'Son of the Most High God'. When Jesus cast them out of the man they took refuge in a nearby herd of pigs, which stampeded into the sea.

As in the instance just given, Jesus sometimes cured simply with a word of command. Sometimes however he employed physical methods. Asked to heal a man who was deaf and who had an impediment in his speech, he put his fingers in the man's ears and touched his tongue with spittle. In the course of healing a blind man he spat on his eyes and laid his hands on him. When the man's sight returned only partially he again laid hands on him to complete the cure.

Jesus possessed a power which other people's faith could draw upon. One day, as he was moving among a dense crowd, a woman who had suffered from bleeding for twelve years and whom doctors had been quite unable to help, broke Jewish laws which forbade her to come close to other people, and touched his cloak. Immediately she was cured. Jesus realised that power had left him, and asked who had touched him. Full of fear, the woman came forward and confessed what she had done. Jesus responded: 'My daughter, your faith has healed you. Go in peace'.

In Jerusalem, as in Galilee, Jesus fell foul of the religious authorities because he healed on the Sabbath. Coming across a man who had been paralysed for thirty-eight years, and who had tried unsuccessfully to take advantage of the curative properties of the pool of Bethesda, he commanded him to take up his mattress and walk. The man did so; but, because the healing had been on the Sabbath day, Jesus was challenged about it. His explanation: 'My Father continues to work, and I must work too' gave further offence, because he was seen as making himself equal to God.

Matthew 16.1-4; Mark 5.1-20, 8.22-6, 5.25-34; John 5.1-18

Putting things right with God

In the rational and scientific world of today, we sit uneasily with the idea of miracles. So we try to explain them away as we might try to second-guess the tricks of a magician. But that is to misunderstand the true nature of miracles and why Jesus performed them. After all, if the only reason for a miracle was to heal a sick person why was he so selective amongst all the poverty and sickness that surrounded him? There must be more to it than Jesus wanting to show off his wonder working powers, amazing as they are.

Jesus saw miracles as an important way of teaching, not by shocking people into believing but by giving them a deeper understanding of God. He seems to be concerned less about medical conditions than the suffering of the people whom he is healing; and less about the people he is healing than the reality of God's forgiveness and love which he has come to demonstrate. Jesus came to proclaim the Kingdom of God, a kingdom of peace, healing and right relationships. The miracles, in fact, are the medium of his message.

Healing of a particular case of sickness, then, becomes less important than being in relationship with God. Jesus wasn't just a healer; he was a proclaimer. The healings were merely the by-product of his proclamation. We might like to be healed of our sickness, whatever it might be, but what is far more important is our right relationship with God and with our family, friends and the society in which we live. At the heart of our dis-ease is our distance from God, and our separation from him through sin. To seek forgiveness for our separation from God is the first step along the road to wholeness, healing and peace of mind.

Meditation

Jesus' approach to healing is a help to our prayers for sick and needy people. It is right to pray for the healing of their bodies and for the relief of pain. We should also remember the importance of their relationship to God and that when that is right everything else is put into its true perspective.

Prayer

O God, the source of healing and peace, still our troubled hearts with your shafts of love. Forgive us and make us whole. Amen.

30 Raising the dead

On three recorded occasions during his ministry Jesus brought dead, or apparently dead, people back to life.

Approaching the town of Nain in Galilee he came across the funeral procession of a young man, the only son of a widowed mother. Filled with compassion for her, Jesus laid his hand on the bier, and halted the procession. Then he said: 'Young man, get up'. To the astonishment of the crowd, the man sat up and began to speak; Jesus restored him to his mother.

On another occasion he was approached by the president of a local synagogue, a man called Jairus. He asked him to come and lay hands on his twelve year-old daughter, who was at death's door. Jesus consented, but on the way messengers came to tell him that the girl had died. Nonetheless Jesus continued to the house, and rebuked the mourners, telling them that the girl was only asleep. They laughed at him, but he went into the room where the girl lay, took her hand and told her to get up. She rose at once, and Jesus told her parents to give her a meal.

Some close friends of Jesus - Lazarus and his sisters, Martha and Mary - lived in the village of Bethany near Jerusalem. One day he received an urgent message from the two women to say that Lazarus was very ill; but he did not set out towards Bethany until two days later. By the time he and his disciples reached the village Lazarus had been buried for four days. First Martha and then Mary met Jesus, and claimed that, had he been there, Lazarus would not have died. Jesus responded to Martha by saying: 'I am the resurrection and the life; anyone believing in me will live, even after dying'. Then, deeply moved by the sisters' distress, he asked to be taken to the tomb. He ordered the removal of the stone covering its entrance, prayed briefly, and cried: 'Lazarus, come out'. The dead man emerged still wrapped in his grave-clothes. Jesus commanded: 'Free him, and let him go'.

This miracle caused a major sensation. When they heard of it, the Jewish leadership feared that Jesus would soon attract mass support and impel the Roman occupiers into a violent reaction. The high priest Caiaphas said: 'It is in our interest that one man should die, rather than that the nation should be destroyed'; and from then on the leadership plotted his death.

Luke 7.11-17; Mark 5.21-24, 35-43; John 11.1-53

Putting aside the fear of death

The three stories of Jesus' raising people from the dead present us with a host of questions even more searching than those presented by the miracles of healing. Could such demonstrations of power really happen? Can death ever be reversed? What is the point of such mind-stretching events? Once again, up to a point we have to set aside our 21st century scientific thinking, and seek the message about God and His Kingdom behind these extraordinary stories.

Two of the stories concern young people, the son of the widow of Nain and the daughter of Jairus the leader of the synagogue. Jesus' concern for a young man and a child is significant: in a culture where children had no rights and little value except to their parents, here was Jesus pointing to the special place in God's kingdom which they occupy. God's kingdom is here and now, not when they are dead.

The third story, told by St John, is rather different and full of symbolism. Lazarus was a friend. His illness and his death caused Jesus to weep. Jesus delays his arrival so that three days should pass before he comes. A stone must be rolled from the tomb, and the dramatic raising of Lazarus forms the climax of the narrative. This story has clear parallels with Jesus' own resurrection.

Meditation

These stories are designed to show that Jesus has power over death as well as life. Death is not the end of life. That is a firm conviction of those who follow Jesus Christ. He rose from the dead, raised others from the dead and described himself as 'the resurrection and the life'. Our difficulties arise when we think of life after death only as an extension of this life – in some kind of time and space. But our future life will be as different from this one as the butterfly is to the caterpillar it came from. We need not fear death and pray that by faith in Jesus we may share in his resurrection.

Prayer

Heavenly Father, in whose hands the living and the dead are safe, take our faltering faith and give us increasing confidence in your power to bring to new life all things in heaven and earth.   Amen

31 Nature miracles

Jesus' miracles were not confined to delivering people from sickness and death. Early in his ministry he, his mother and his disciples were guests at a wedding in Cana in Galilee when the supply of wine ran low. Jesus told the house servants to fill some large jars, usually used for ritual washing, with water. When the water was poured out it had turned to wine. The president of the feast commented that the wine was of a better quality than that which had previously been served.

One day when Simon Peter and his friends had spent a fruitless night fishing, Jesus told them to try again. This time they hauled in such a catch that their nets broke and their boats began to sink. Amazed, Peter fell at Jesus' feet, and exclaimed: 'Leave me, Lord, for I am a sinner.' Jesus replied: 'Do not be afraid; from now on you will be catching people.'

After Jesus had spent a day teaching, he and his disciples were crossing the Sea of Galilee when a storm arose. Jesus was asleep in the stern of the boat, but, in fear of death, his disciples aroused him. He rebuked them for their lack of faith, and calmed the wind and the waves with the words: 'Peace! Be still!' . In awe the disciples commented: 'Who can this man be? Even the wind and the sea obey him.'

On one occasion a great crowd gathered to hear him in a desert place. As evening drew on, his disciples suggested the people should go away and buy food. Jesus said 'You give them something to eat.' The disciples replied that they had no more than five loaves and two fishes. Nevertheless Jesus commanded the crowd to sit down in groups, blessed the food, and divided it. Not only was there sufficient for the five thousand who were there, but twelve baskets of fragments were collected afterwards.

After this miracle he sent his disciples ahead of him by boat across Lake Galilee, while he remained behind to pray. As the boat struggled against the wind in the darkness of the night, the disciples saw Jesus walking past them on the water. Thinking it was a ghost, they were terrified and cried out. He reassured them, and, as he joined them in the boat, the wind died away.

John 2.1-12; Luke 5.1-11; Mark 4.35-41, 6.30-52

Signs of God's power and unlimited generosity

Unlike those miracles in the previous sections, these are about groups rather than individuals. They neither heal nor raise from the dead but each one is full of meaning to demonstrate Jesus's power to love and to save. Once again we lay aside our scientific presuppositions and look at each one for its meaning to our faith.

The miracle at Cana, where Jesus turned water into wine, demonstrates Jesus's unlimited love and generosity and speaks of the Marriage Feast as a foretaste of the everlasting banquet of the Kingdom.

The miraculous catch of fish touches the everyday life of his friends and is a sign of the endless resources which God has to offer. It is also an indication of what he expects of his disciples in their work of telling people about Him.

The stilling of the storm on Galilee is a sign of Jesus's power over natural forces as well as being a wonderfully symbolic description of Jesus's dealing with our faltering faith. Similarly Jesus' walking on the water is a sign of encouragement to his followers that he is master of the wind, the waves and the storm.

Finally, the feeding of the five thousand is a sign of Jesus's power to break bread to feed and satisfy unlimited numbers of people. For many it has also been a reminder of Jesus' use of bread and wine in the Last Supper and the strength that has brought to Christians down the ages in the Holy Communion or the Mass.

Meditation

These signs demonstrate powerfully who Jesus is. He is a man like one of us, yet he has power beyond nature. In his person, the Kingdom of God is breaking into our physical world. As we make our way as followers of Jesus Christ can we sense His Kingdom breaking into our lives and opening our eyes to His presence all around us?

Prayer

O God, maker of our world in all its beauty and fragility, hear our prayer for the renewal of all creation in Jesus Christ.   Amen

32 Who is Jesus?

From the earliest days of his ministry there was speculation about how Jesus fitted into Jewish religious expectations.

When he and his disciples were in the territory to the north of the Sea of Galilee, on the way to the villages of Caesarea Philippi, he asked what people were saying about him. The disciples replied that some thought that he was John the Baptist or Elijah come again, some that he was a prophet. When he asked them who they thought he was, Peter replied: 'You are the Messiah'. Jesus accepted the title, but ordered his disciples to say nothing about it in public. Then he began to teach them that he was a Messiah who must endure suffering and rejection; who would be put to death and then rise again. Peter found this teaching hard to accept. He remonstrated with Jesus, who rebuked him severely for thinking in human rather than in divine terms. He told the disciples that following him involved sharing his suffering: 'Anyone who wants to save his life will lose it, but anyone who loses his life for my sake, and for the sake of the good news I bring, will save it'.

Some days later Jesus took Peter, James and John up a mountain. There they saw him transfigured; his clothes became dazzling white, and glory shone around him. Moses and Elijah appeared to them and spoke with Jesus. The disciples were awe-struck and terrified. Then a cloud overshadowed them, and a voice from heaven declared: 'This is my beloved son; listen to him'; at that the vision disappeared. Afterwards, as they descended the hillside, Jesus told the disciples to say nothing about what had happened until he had risen from the dead, a concept they found difficult to grasp. They asked him what the Scriptures meant by saying that Elijah must come first, to set everything right. Jesus replied that Elijah had already come, in the person of John the Baptist.

When they rejoined the other disciples, they found them surrounded by a crowd arguing with them over their failure to cure an epileptic boy. Jesus talked with the boy's father who described the terrible effects of his son's illness and then cried: 'Lord I believe; help my unbelief'. Jesus cured the boy, and later told his disciples that some illnesses would respond only to prayer.

Mark 8.27-9.27; Matthew 11.14

Jesus reveals who he is

Who do we think Jesus is? There came a moment in the unfolding story when Jesus had to challenge his closest disciples to answer this question, just as there comes a moment in each of our lives when we must face it too.

He said to them, "Who do you say that I am?" Peter, the impulsive one, came out with the answer, "You are the Messiah." He of all the disciples could see in Jesus the long-awaited saviour. But immediately Jesus warned them all of the suffering, indignity and danger that this would mean. For him it would mean death. For many of his followers over the centuries, being loyal to their faith has literally cost them their lives. But all Christians have understood this saying as meaning for them a turning back (a 'dying') from a self centred life in order to find your true self in a life lived for others.

The story of the Transfiguration acts this teaching out. In the sight of Peter, James and John, Jesus's body is filled with heavenly light and he is transfigured before them, while a voice is heard affirming, "This is my Son, the Beloved." It is as though his human body is for a moment seen in all its Godly glory, his humanity and his divinity are for the first time seen as inseparable. For Jesus, this was an intimate preparation for crucifixion and all that would flow from that. For his watching followers it was both a challenge to their faith and an encouragement to stay with him.

Meditation

It is the person of Christ who challenges us with the question, "Who do you say that I am?" and we have to find an answer for ourselves. If we are to answer, "You are the Messiah," then are we prepared for God to take our lives and use them?

The Jesus Prayer

Lord Jesus Christ, Son of the Living God, have mercy on me a sinner. Amen

33 Jesus' true nature

It was not until Jesus had risen from the dead that his followers began fully to understand his true nature. What that nature was is explained by John in his description of Jesus' ministry. His book begins by asserting that the Word, the creative activity of God through all eternity, was made flesh in the person of Jesus. His own people did not accept him, but to everyone who did accept him he gave the right to become a child of God. The Law was given through Moses; but grace and truth came through Jesus Christ.

In several passages John writes about Jesus' claims about himself. For example, one evening Nicodemus, a leading Pharisee, visited him. He told Jesus that he believed him to be a teacher sent by God. Jesus responded by saying that only those who are born again through water and the Spirit can see the kingdom of God. 'How is that possible?' asked Nicodemus. Jesus rebuked him, a Jewish teacher, for his inability to understand the truth. Then he claimed a special relationship with, and a special mission from, God. He said: 'God loved the world so much that he sent his only Son, so that everyone who has faith in him should not perish but have eternal life. God did not send his Son to judge the world, but to save it.'

On another occasion Jesus engaged in conversation with a Samaritan woman who came to draw water at a well. She was astonished when Jesus asked her for a drink, because there was deep hostility between Jews and Samaritans. But Jesus said: 'If you only understood the gifts of God, and who is asking you for a drink, you would have asked him, and he would have given you living water. Everyone who drinks ordinary water will be thirsty again, but whoever drinks the water I offer will never be thirsty. The water I give will be a spring giving eternal life.'

At first the woman misunderstood what was being said to her, and Jesus had to clear away misconceptions arising from her own sinfulness and from the controversies dividing Samaritans from Jews. Then he told her that he was in fact the Messiah. The woman told the people of her village what Jesus had said. He stayed there for two days and many of them became convinced that he was the Saviour of the world.

John 1.1-18, 3.1-21, 4.1-42

Making a difference

We describe the nature of Jesus as "God incarnate", God in Jesus taking on human flesh and becoming a human being like one of us. It is a startling, shocking, idea that Jesus could lay aside his heavenly glory and share our human nature. Jesus as God incarnate diminishes the idea of a great and mighty God. But he brings God down to our level and allows us to reach God, and speak to him "as a person speaks with a friend."

We may share in this One who is wholly God and truly human, this Jesus, by being "born again by water and the Spirit" as Jesus said to Nicodemus. The Christian Church sees this second birth as taking place in the sacrament of Baptism. As we are each washed in the water of Baptism we are born again in Jesus Christ, united with him in his death and resurrection, and given the gift of his Holy Spirit. This is the water which "will be a spring giving eternal life" which Jesus described to the Samaritan woman at the well. It assures us of our inheritance of life for ever with God.

Everyone who has faith in Jesus "should not perish, but have eternal life." Placing our faith in Jesus re-orders our life in God's direction so starting a new kind of life with Jesus Christ.

Meditation

It can be a problem turning words like these into action so that they make a difference to our lives. If we trivialise it or think of it only in emotional terms, we will be disappointed, perhaps even disillusioned. But if we think of it as taking a turning at a cross roads and simply the beginning of a new life's journey then we can begin. It is an act involving emotion, intellect and will. It begins in a different way for each individual. It makes all the difference to us and our life in the world.

34 On the way to Jerusalem

The time came for Jesus to make his final visit to Jerusalem. On the way he continued to warn his disciples of the fate which awaited him; but they continued to fail to understand him, even though they saw him being fiercely critical of the Jewish leadership and protective of people whom most Jews despised. He accused the Pharisees, the strictest of all Jews in their observance, of hypocrisy. This was because, although the Pharisees kept the outward requirements of the Jewish Law rigorously, they disregarded its more profound requirements of justice and love. He claimed that the Pharisees and the teachers of the Law oppressed ordinary people and persecuted those who taught new religious truth, as he did.

On the journey Jesus constantly challenged the assumptions of those who heard him or offered him hospitality. Dining with a Pharisee, and seeing the competition among the guests for a place of honour, he used the occasion to teach that God will exalt the humble, and humble those who seek to be among the highest. He said hospitality should be offered, not to friends or well-off neighbours, but to those who are unable to return it. The host's reward would come when the righteous rise from the dead.

In another implied rebuke to his own people he told a story of guests refusing, with a variety of excuses, an invitation to a feast. In anger the host filled his house with the poor and maimed; there was no longer any room for those first invited.

As they were approaching the town of Jericho a blind beggar, using a form of address reserved to the Messiah, shouted out to him: 'Jesus, Son of David, have pity on me'. People told him to be quiet, but he continued shouting until Jesus sent for him and restored his sight.

When Jesus arrived in Jericho itself a man named Zacchaeus, a wealthy tax-gatherer, climbed a tree in order to see him amidst the crowds. Observing him, Jesus invited himself to dinner at his house. During the meal Zacchaeus vowed to give half his possessions to the poor and to recompense everyone he had defrauded. Jesus rejoiced, saying: 'Today salvation has come to this family. I have come to seek and to save those who are lost'.

Luke 9.51, 11.37-52, 14.7-24, 18.31-19.10

The meaning of salvation for all

The tension is building. Jesus was preparing for the end of the story as he set his face towards Jerusalem where his destiny is to be fulfilled. The teaching he gave centred on the promise of the new Kingdom which would shed fresh light on the true meaning of God's law. A new way of living, emphasising God's love and forgiveness, was going to replace the old burdensome ways of interpreting the law.

The parable of the Great Banquet is a characteristic example of this. Those who had originally been invited to the banquet made excuses not to come. In anger at this refusal, the owner of the house ordered that the banquet was to be thrown open to the poor, the crippled, the blind and the lame who were to be welcomed in. In the coming Kingdom, it is the outcasts of society who will be welcome. The accepted norms of society will be overturned.

Zacchaeus was despised because of his association with the detested Roman occupation and because he was suspected of feathering his own pocket at the people's expense. He was therefore a social outcast. Was it just curiosity or a spiritual hunger which made him search for a glimpse of Jesus? The crowd must have been shocked that Jesus then took the initiative and brought about a change of heart, what Jesus calls 'salvation', in Zacchaeus.

Meditation

Salvation is a rather wonderful word. It has meanings which are to do with healing wounds and saving from disease or harm. Saving from disaster, as a lifeboat crew might do, has a noble meaning often involving sacrifice or putting oneself in danger to accomplish it. In Christian terms salvation is that which Christ brings to rescue us, heal us and set us on a new path of life. If Jesus came to visit our house, as he did with Zacchaeus what would be our reaction?

Prayer

O Lord God, lover of souls, correct and heal our disordered lives that we may serve you in Spirit and in Truth.   Amen.

35 Arrival at Jerusalem

As Jesus and his disciples approached Jerusalem James and John asked a favour: that, when Jesus came into his kingdom, they might sit on his right and his left. Jesus asked them if they were able to face what faced him; they said they were. Jesus told them that they would indeed suffer as he was going to, but that the highest places in his kingdom were not his to give. When the other disciples heard about this conversation they were indignant; so Jesus explained to them that any of his followers who wanted to be great must be prepared to serve as he was doing, giving his life as a ransom for others.

Just outside Jerusalem Jesus sent two of his disciples into a nearby village and told them to bring back a donkey which they would find tethered there. If they were challenged they were to say: 'The Master needs it'. They did as they had been told, and, when they had brought the donkey, they spread their cloaks on it. Other followers spread their garments and greenery from the fields on the road in front of Jesus, and as he rode into Jerusalem crowds acclaimed him, waving palm branches and shouting: 'Praise God! God bless him who comes in the name of the Lord! God bless the kingdom of our father King David which is to come!' So a prophecy of Zechariah was fulfilled.

The next day Jesus went into the Temple and drove out those who bought and sold there. He declared that the Temple should be a house of prayer but that it had been turned into a den of thieves. The authorities wanted to arrest him, but they were frightened of the crowds who gathered round him and who were spellbound by his teaching.

One evening Jesus was eating in a friend's house in Bethany where he was staying. A woman came in with a jar of costly perfume and anointed him with it. Some of the guests were indignant, saying that the perfume could have been sold and the money given to the poor. But Jesus defended the woman, saying: 'You can help the poor at any time, but, by anointing me, this woman has prepared my body for burial.'

After this Judas Iscariot went to the Jewish authorities and offered to hand Jesus over to them. He was promised thirty pieces of silver to betray him. He began to plan how an arrest could be contrived.

Mark 10.32-45, 11.1-12, 15-19, 14.1-11;
John 12.13; Matthew 21.5, 26.14-16

Destination and destiny

Jesus's entry into Jerusalem was marked by signs of triumph – he rode into town to the waving of banners and the crowds acclaimed him king. But his steed was a donkey, a beast of burden, the banners were just tree branches and the crowd an easily roused group of curious people. Jesus's triumph was the victory of humility. His disciples found it hard to understand that this way was not the way of success but of service and sacrifice.

But Jesus had chosen a symbolic way to take possession of his heritage. He entered the Temple and, in anger at the hypocrisy and empty religion he found there, he drove out those who bought and sold the Temple currency and exploit the religious zeal of the people. His cry, "My house shall be a house of prayer," is a reminder to us of the priority of the honesty and integrity of true religion. Jesus is saying that what counts is our relationship with God not the commercialisation of formalised religion.

Back in Bethany with his friends Jesus was prepared for the final struggle by being anointed with precious oil. This costly act of reverence by a woman was a sign of the love and affirmation of his heavenly Father, as well as being a symbol of the anointing of his body after death. It raises the question of whether we can ever be too extravagant in what we offer to God just as he gave his everything for us.

These events all led in one direction: to Jesus's final sacrifice.

Meditation

Can we, in our imagination, picture his journey and feel his tension and his apprehension at the approaching destiny?

Prayer

O heavenly Father, we would share with your Son Jesus the suffering of his journey into Jerusalem. Open our hearts to the knowledge of his pain that we may know the depth of his suffering and learn of its power to save and to heal.   Amen.

36 Jesus teaches in the Temple

As the festival of the Passover approached Jesus went daily to the Temple, and taught believers, the sceptical, and the hostile. One day he told a parable about a man who planted a vineyard and let it out to tenants. When he sent servants to collect his share of the harvest, the tenants ill-treated them, beating some and killing others. Finally the owner sent his son in the hope that he, at least, would be treated with respect. The tenants, recognising him as the heir and wishing to take the vineyard for themselves, killed him too. 'How would the owner react?' Jesus asked his hearers. 'By killing the tenants and giving the vineyard to others.'

The Jewish leaders realised that this story was aimed at them - they were the tenants in the story. They would have liked to arrest Jesus, but they were frightened of the crowd's reaction. Instead they sent questioners to trap him into indiscretion. He was asked whether it was right to pay taxes to the Roman Emperor or not. Jesus asked to see a silver coin and enquired whose image was upon it. To the reply: 'The Emperor's', he rejoined: 'Give to the Emperor what is the Emperor's and to God what is God's.'

A group of leading Jews, the Sadducees, did not believe in the resurrection of the dead, so some of them told Jesus a story about a woman who, in order to fulfil the requirements of the Jewish law, married seven brothers in succession, in the vain hope of producing an heir. 'To which of them,' they asked, 'would she be married when the dead rise?' Jesus replied: 'There is no marriage after the resurrection of the dead; but how can you deny that the dead will rise? The God of Abraham and Isaac and Jacob is the God of the living, not of the dead.'

Asked what the foremost commandment was, Jesus replied that there were two greater than all the others. The first is 'Hear, O Israel, the Lord our God is one Lord, and you must love the Lord your God with all your heart, with all your soul, with all your mind and with all your strength'. The second is: 'You must love your neighbour as yourself'.

Mark 11.27-12.34

The Establishment and Jesus

During his last week, Jesus travelled daily to the Temple in Jerusalem to teach. There he met with Temple officials, Pharisees and Sadducees who posed testing questions in an attempt to compromise him and enable them to arrest him. Conflict is growing between the threatened establishment figures, with their own inflexibilities, and Jesus' new message of a religion which touched heart and mind and soul.

One test was about Roman taxes. Should taxes be paid to the hated Roman authorities? If he answered "No" he would be guilty of treason towards Rome; if he answered "Yes" he would be seen as a Roman collaborator. He responded in a way that silenced his questioners and helped them to reflect on the nature of God's Kingdom.

Another conflict was with the Sadducees. They were an influential element in Jewish society at the time of Jesus. Challenging their narrow-minded religion, he effectively said 'Never mind your trick questions, why don't you have faith in the living God who offers eternal life to all?'

They persisted with - 'So what's the law about then? Which is the most important law?' Jesus' reply strips the Law down to essentials. 'Love God'(not just obey him) which implied a living relationship with him. 'Love your neighbour' knowing that he, like you, is worthy of love. Our love is to reflect the indiscriminate love which God has for us.

Meditation

Here we see Jesus at the height of his power, teaching with skill and confidence, knowing, no doubt, that his time was running out. What would it have felt like for us to be there to hear him? Would we have been sympathetic, sceptical, or inspired?

Prayer

God of Love come and fill the hearts of your faithful people, and kindle in them the fire of your love. For Jesus Christ's sake,   Amen.

37 Teaching about judgement

During the last weeks of his ministry Jesus spoke at length about difficult times to come and about the necessity of being prepared for God's judgment.

When his disciples admired the Temple building, he prophesied that it would be destroyed. He taught that times of human and natural disaster were coming; that his followers would be brought before courts and be beaten and executed; and that, in the face of danger, the only recourse would be to instant flight. During the times of turmoil there would be many false prophets and Messiahs, but finally the Son of Man - he himself - would appear to gather to himself those who had been faithful to him. Only God knew when this event would occur, and so Jesus' followers must be constantly ready and constantly on the watch.

To illustrate this teaching, he told a parable about a man going abroad and entrusting three of his servants with portions of his capital. On his return he summoned them to give account of themselves. Two of the servants had doubled their investments; he gave them extra responsibility and admitted them to his high favour. The servant to whom he had entrusted the least had done least with it; he simply returned the original sum he had been given. This dereliction of duty angered his master; he gave the investment to the servant who had earned most, and dismissed the idle one from his service. Jesus concluded: 'Everyone who has will be given much more; but he who has not will be deprived of even the little he possesses.'

In another parable Jesus described the Son of Man coming with his angels, sitting on the throne of judgment, and dividing humanity into two groups, the sheep and the goats. He set the sheep on his right and the goats on his left. He said to those on his right: 'Come, enter into God's kingdom. You fed me when I was hungry, gave me drink, hospitality, and clothing when I was in need, and visited me when I was sick and in prison.' Those to whom he spoke were surprised, and asked him when they had helped him. The Son of Man replied: 'Whatever you did to help anyone, however insignificant, you did for me.' But to those on his left he said: 'Because you have failed to help those in need, you have failed to help me.' They were sent away to eternal punishment, while the righteous entered eternal life.

Mark 13; Matthew 25.14–46

Behaviour has its consequences

The concept of the Day of Judgement is both frightening and comforting. Frightening because it suggests that hell is as real an alternative as heaven and that in the end we will not escape God's judgement on our conduct in this life; comforting because it suggests that Jesus will finally come again to complete what he has begun, putting to right the world and all that is wrong in it.

Jesus tells many parables about Judgement. Some are harvest parables which describe the growth of the wheat until it is cut down at harvest time. Some are wedding-banquet parables which describe the long-awaited arrival of the bridegroom. Others are Second Coming parables which describe a king or a landowner who goes away for a long time and eventually returns to settle accounts with his tenants.

The parable of the sheep and the goats falls into the last category. It has a heaven versus hell setting, a judgement seat, a separation of the blessed from the cursed and a glimpse of reward or punishment. This is the parable which was frequently painted on the chancel arch of medieval churches, as a regular reminder to worshippers how they should conduct their lives. Behaviour does have its consequences.

Behind the idea of judgement lies the objective reality of sin. Our sins are those actions we do, knowingly or unknowingly, which are wrong and separate us from God's love. In that way we create a hell for ourselves. But the central message of the Christian faith is that no one is beyond the reach of God who will forgive us and restore us as we seek to find him.

Meditation

Does the idea of Judgement comfort us more than it disturbs us?

Prayer

O God, in whom we live and move and have our being, deliver us we pray from those sins which have separated us from you, in Jesus Christ.   Amen.

38 The Last Supper

On the day before he died, Jesus ate with his disciples in the upper room of a house in Jerusalem. During the meal he blessed and broke bread, gave it to his disciples and said: 'This is my body given for you. Do this in memory of me'. After supper he shared a cup of wine with them, saying: 'This cup, poured out for you, is the new covenant sealed by my blood. Whenever you drink it, do this in memory of me.'

Jesus then warned Peter that he would undergo a time of trial. In reply Peter exclaimed: 'Lord, I am willing to go to prison and to death with you!' Jesus replied: 'You will deny me three times before the cock crows tomorrow.'

During the meal he washed the feet of his disciples, a duty usually undertaken by a slave. He told them that if he, their teacher and Lord, was prepared to serve them they ought to be prepared to serve each other in the same way. Then, in great distress, he said that one of the disciples was going to betray him. Later Judas left the meal for that very purpose, without the other disciples realising what his intention was.

After Judas had left, Jesus spoke at length with the eleven, preparing them for what lay ahead. In earlier teaching he had called himself the bread of life, the light of the world, the good shepherd, and the resurrection and the life. Now he told them that he was the way, the truth and the life and that the way to God the Father lay through him. He described himself as the true vine; only branches which remain united with the vine can bear fruit. Commanding them to love each other as he had loved them, he said that the highest expression of love was to lay down one's life for one's friends. He warned them to expect hatred and persecution, but promised them the gift of the Holy Spirit, who would enable them to remember what they had been taught and who would guide them into further truth. Finally he prayed for those whom God had called out of the world into union with himself. He asked that they might share his joy and glory, and be one in him.

Luke 22.1-20; 1 Corinthians 11.24-25; John 13-17

Jesus – ever present

The Last Supper means many things. It is the coming together in fellowship of all Jesus' disciples, including Judas who betrayed him, for the last time. It honours Jewish tradition in the manner of the Passover meal; it looks back to the blessings God has granted in delivering the Jewish people from slavery in Egypt and looks forward to the final deliverance in the coming Resurrection. It is the opportunity for Jesus to institute the Holy Communion, and it is a preparation for the sacrifice which will inevitably follow.

All these thoughts would have been in Jesus' mind as he shared this supper with his disciples. He followed Passover custom and took the bread and the cup. As he did so, he gave them a new meaning. "This bread is my body; this cup is my blood." Now the bread of affliction and the cup of blessing were actually to be Jesus himself, so that in this sacred meal his followers could actually share in him. More than this, he said, "Do this in remembrance of me." The Church of Christ has always remembered this, and has broken bread and shared wine in remembrance of Jesus Christ ever since.

The Last Supper was indeed a final shared meal, and was a meal of sorrow. But it was also the institution of a promise which will never be broken: that Jesus will always be present with us in the bread and wine of the Last Supper, otherwise called The Lord's Supper, the Eucharist, the Holy Communion or the Mass. Jesus validated this promise in his crucifixion and resurrection.

Meditation

Christian people will always wish to be there when the Holy Communion is celebrated, for by sharing in this meal we renew our fellowship with Jesus and our promise to go on following him.

Prayer

Be round our every table, Lord, and especially when we remember that your body was broken and your blood outpoured for the sake of the whole world.   Amen

39 The Garden of Gethsemane

After leaving the upper room, Jesus led his disciples to the Mount of Olives just outside Jerusalem. When they reached a place called Gethsemane he took Peter, James and John, and went apart from the other disciples to pray. In great distress he said to the three disciples: 'My heart is breaking with grief; stay here and watch with me.' Going a little further away, he threw himself to the ground and prayed that he might be spared what was to come. His prayer was: 'Father, everything is possible for you; take this cup from me. Yet not my will but yours be done.'

Returning to his friends he found them asleep. He urged them to stay awake and to pray that they might be delivered from temptation. Nonetheless they fell asleep twice more. As he roused them for the third time, an armed crowd, sent by the Jewish authorities and guided by Judas, arrived.

Judas had told those with him: 'Arrest the man whom I kiss, and lead him away.' Going up to Jesus he said 'Rabbi!' and kissed him. Those with Judas seized Jesus, and there was a brief struggle during which one of the high priest's servants lost an ear. Jesus touched and healed him, and asked: 'Do you think I am a robber, that you come to arrest me with swords and cudgels? I taught in the Temple daily and you left me alone there. However let the Scriptures be fulfilled.' Then all his disciples deserted him and ran away.

After his arrest Jesus was taken to the house of the High Priest Caiaphas. Peter followed at a distance, and joined a group sitting by a fire in the courtyard. A serving maid stared at him and said 'This man was with them.' Peter replied: 'I do not know him.' As the night wore on, two other people accused him of being a companion of Jesus, one of them pointing out that his accent indicated that he came from Galilee; but each time he denied it strongly. Just after his third denial the cock crew. Jesus turned and looked at Peter, who remembered Jesus' prophecy and his own pledge of the previous evening. He went outside and wept bitterly.

Mark 14.26-50; Luke 22.51-62

Agony and tears

The Garden of Gethsemane is still there. The trees on the Mount of Olives are reputed to be the descendants of those which Jesus walked amongst. The stone on which Jesus prayed is still there. There is a reality, an earthiness, about the basis of the Christian faith which is compelling. It is about a living person and we can still touch the things which he touched.

The reality is more than physical. It probes the far reaches of human experience: despair as well as hope; agony as well as ecstasy; bitter tears as well as infectious laughter. Jesus' agony and tears in Gethsemane take us into the intimate inner struggles of the Son of God experiencing all the emotions of a human being. His human instincts are to ask for an escape from what lies before him. But his perfect love puts God's will first. We can hear the echoes of that in our own inner struggles which want to do the right thing, while there remains a strong craving for escape and comfort.

We often take the easy way – like the disciples in this story who wanted to sleep, run away or blatantly deny they knew anything of Jesus. The tides and fashions of 21st century society present us with all the attractions of power, of the easy life, of self-indulgence, of fulfilling every desire. Meanwhile half the world still starves, violence is still fearfully common, and the planet itself is still vulnerable to self-destruction. The battle which Jesus wept about is still on.

Meditation

Some moments require silence. Words seem empty. The Gethsemane moment was like that. The struggle between good and evil in the world comes to a climax here and then on the Cross. Jesus must still weep for the world because the tension between creative goodness and destructive evil still goes on. But Jesus is there. Just as he is there when we struggle with our personal temptations, weaknesses and efforts to be like Him. Can we recall times of struggle in our own experience when he has been there for us?

Prayer

Father, keep me strong when the pressure is on,

Keep me real amongst the fantasies,

Keep me faithful to you, like Jesus Christ, my Lord.   *Amen*

40 The trials of Jesus

During the night Jesus' guards insulted and tormented him. They blindfolded and beat him, saying mockingly: 'If you are a prophet, tell us who hit you'. When morning came Jesus was brought before the Jewish Governing Council, which consisted of the chief priests, elders and teachers of the Law. 'Tell us,' they said, 'if you are the Messiah, the Son of God'. His reply, 'It is you who say that I am', was regarded as sufficient evidence for his condemnation for blasphemy. He was taken before Pontius Pilate, the Roman governor, and accused of claiming to be King of the Jews and thus of subverting Roman rule. After interrogating him Pilate concluded he had done nothing wrong, and was inclined to release him. When however he discovered that Jesus came from Galilee, he sent him to be judged by the ruler of that province, Herod son of Herod the Great, who happened to be in Jerusalem.

Herod had heard a great deal about Jesus and had long wanted to meet him. He questioned him at length, but Jesus refused to reply. Eventually Herod sent him back to Pilate arrayed in a gorgeous robe, thereby making up a quarrel between them.

Pilate still believed that Jesus was being falsely accused, and his wife sent him a message to the same effect. So he decided to take advantage of a custom by which a prisoner chosen by the people was released at Passover-tide. He was holding another well-known prisoner whose name was Jesus Barabbas, and he asked the crowd which had gathered: 'Which one would you like me to release - Jesus Barabbas or Jesus who is called the Messiah?' The chief priests and elders had worked on the crowd, so they responded 'Barabbas'. 'What then am I to do with Jesus called Messiah?' asked Pilate. The reply came repeatedly and with increasing emphasis: 'Crucify him!'

When Pilate saw that his efforts to save Jesus were fruitless, and that there was a danger of a riot breaking out, he took water and washed his hands, saying; 'My hands are clean of this man's blood'. He released Barabbas and had Jesus flogged; then he handed him over to be crucified. The soldiers made sport of him, stripping him, dressing him in a scarlet cloak, and putting a reed in his hand and a crown of thorns on his head. They paid him mock homage, spat upon him, and beat him. Then they put on his clothes again, and led him away.

Luke 22.63-23.12; Matthew 27.15-31

Stripped of dignity yet true to himself

The torture and crucifixion of Jesus actually happened and such is the tragedy of it all that it demands our attention and response.

The Jewish guard, and later the Roman soldiers, made a sport of taking any human dignity from Jesus. They took their cue from their worried leaders; the Jews because they feared a threat to their religious authority; the Romans because they sensed a threat to their political authority. In both cases the issue was power, considered to be finite so that the more power one person has the less the other has. So the hesitancy of the High Priest, Pilate and Herod is the reaction of weak leaders, fearing subversion. They were not necessarily bad people but weak in that they sacrificed truth for expediency.

This lack of principle set against Jesus' sublime integrity was what took him to the cross and exemplified the timeless moral battle in the world. The conflict between power grabbing for supremacy and power sharing in servanthood remains the core question between nations and between individuals.

Meditation

Deliberate acts of evil are bad enough but when righteous people neglect to stand up for truth and right it seems to be even worse. We kneel under the Cross and have to ask ourselves whether we can just do nothing. How can we overcome our apathy which defeats our best intentions?

Prayer

Lord God, I praise you for the glory of human nature that is in Jesus. Build his spirit within me and give me courage to be on the side of truth.   Amen

41 The Crucifixion

By then Jesus was too weak to carry his cross to the place of execution, so the soldiers compelled a man named Simon from Cyrene in North Africa to carry it for him. Among the great crowd which followed him were many women, who wept for him. Jesus told them to weep for themselves and for their children because dreadful times were coming.

When they reached the place called 'The Skull' the soldiers crucified him and two criminals, one of them on his right and one on his left. Jesus said: 'Father forgive them; they do not know what they are doing.' Above his head was an inscription saying 'The King of the Jews'. The soldiers shared out his clothes by casting lots; they and the crowd, which included Jewish leaders, jeered at him, saying: 'He saved other people; now let him save himself if he really is God's chosen Messiah'. Even one of the criminals crucified with him joined in the taunting; but the other reproached him, saying: 'We are getting what we deserve, but this man has done nothing wrong'. Then he said to Jesus: 'Remember me when you inherit your kingdom'. Jesus replied: 'Today you will be with me in Paradise'.

From midday darkness fell until three o'clock in the afternoon. Then Jesus shouted: 'My God, my God, why have you deserted me?' Some of the bystanders thought he was calling upon Elijah; one of them offered him wine in a sponge held on the end of a stick, and said: 'Let's see if Elijah will come and help him'. Jesus then gave another loud cry and died; and at that very moment the curtain dividing the Holy of Holies from the rest of the Temple building was torn in two. When the Roman officer who had supervised the execution saw how Jesus had died he said: 'This man was really God's Son'.

The day was a Friday, the eve of the Sabbath, and the Jews were anxious that the bodies should not remain on the crosses once the Sabbath had begun. Pilate therefore agreed that the legs of the condemned men should be broken, to hasten their deaths. This was done in the cases of the two criminals but when the soldiers came to Jesus they found he was already dead. They did not break his legs, but one of them thrust a spear into his side, causing a flow of blood and water.

Luke 23.26-43; Mark 15.33-39; John 19.31-37

Deliverance from evil

In previous parts of The 100 Minute Bible one section may have summarised decades or whole books of the Bible. Now we find five sections devoted to three days. That is because we are at the crucial heart of the Christian faith. The Cross on which Jesus died has become the symbol of faith for millions of people, recognised high on magnificent buildings, held by the dying, bejewelled in high fashion, etched on prison walls. This is extraordinary when crucifixion was common in the first century Roman Empire.

At the demand of a hysterical crowd Jesus took the place of a criminal. His (sham) trial became a popular sideshow when Jerusalem was crowded for the religious festival of Passover. Jesus, hanging on the cross, even speaks of forgiveness to the soldiers and of paradise to one of the thieves who were crucified with him.

Focussed on the cross, therefore, are the universal and timeless questions about innocent suffering, oppressed peoples and the malicious use of power. Equally, intensely personal issues are raised about selfishness, wrongdoing and guilt. Deliverance and forgiveness are the deep needs of nations and of individuals.

Jesus, even whilst experiencing the ultimate of human vulnerability – death – declares himself to be truly human and subject to all the inhumanities that can be thrown at him. He, innocently and unjustly, takes the consequences of a world gone wrong. "My God, my God why have you forsaken me?" Yet in offering forgiveness to the Roman soldiers and those being crucified beside him he makes a statement about unconditional love and forgiveness.

Meditation

Even though Jesus' ultimate sacrifice has shown the way in which evil is defeated, the battle between good and evil continues throughout the world. How can we play our part in making this truth known so that everyone may claim that deliverance and be free of the bondage of evil?

Prayer

Lord, make me understand it. Help me to take it in: what it meant to you, the Holy One, to take away my sin.   *Amen*

42 Jesus rises from the dead

That Friday evening Joseph of Arimathaea, a member of the Jewish Governing Council but also a follower of Jesus, asked Pilate if he might have Jesus' body. Once Pilate had given permission, the body was taken down from the cross and wrapped in a linen sheet. Then it was laid in a tomb cut out of the rock, which Joseph had prepared for himself, and a large stone was rolled in front of it. Some of the women who had witnessed the crucifixion watched over the grave.

The next day the Jewish leaders asked Pilate if they could protect the tomb with a guard, lest the disciples should come, steal the body and then falsely claim that Jesus had risen from the dead. Pilate agreed to their request, and the tomb was sealed and guarded.

At daybreak on Sunday, two days later, Mary Magdalene and another Mary, two of the women who had watched over the tomb, visited it again. Suddenly there was a violent earthquake and an angel, descending from heaven, rolled away the stone in front of the tomb, and sat upon it. He said to the women: 'Do not be afraid. Jesus has been raised and is going before you to Galilee. Go quickly, and tell his disciples.'

As the women hurried away in awe and joy they were met by Jesus himself. They knelt before him; he told them to continue with their errand and to deliver the message the angel had given them. Meanwhile the guards at the tomb, who had been overcome with fear when the angel appeared, returned to the Jewish leaders and told them what had happened. The leaders bribed them to say that the disciples had come by night and stolen the body; and this story was circulated widely.

Later that day two downcast followers of Jesus were walking to the village of Emmaus, seven miles from Jerusalem. Jesus joined them on the road, but they did not recognise him. He asked the reason for their sadness, and they told him of all that had recently occurred in Jerusalem. In response he used the Scriptures to explain that it was necessary for the Messiah to suffer before being glorified. When the travellers reached their home they invited him in; and, as he blessed and broke bread, they realised who he was. Then he disappeared, and they immediately set off back to Jerusalem to tell the other disciples what they had seen and heard.

Matthew 27.37-28.15; Luke 24.13-33

Resurrection : Letting go : New life

Jesus was dead and His body lay in a tomb. But the Jewish leaders still remained anxious lest the tomb became the focus of attention of Jesus's followers. So they asked that the tomb be closely guarded.

Alarmed that the body had 'disappeared', the Jewish authorities bribed the guards to say that Jesus's disciples had stolen the body because the gossip-mongers would have had a field day with conspiracy theories. Conflicting stories about the disappearance of the body would have abounded and the true story would have been only one among many.

There is, however, no doubt from the gospel stories that Jesus rose, bodily, from the dead. Jesus was seen in a variety of different places and circumstances and by diverse kinds of people. The fact that this experience also changed the lives of the disciples is further evidence that something profound and lasting happened at the resurrection. The story of the two disciples on the road to Emmaus may have been about a husband and wife for whom despondency, bewilderment and grief turn into a new energy of exhilaration and hope, as Jesus was recognised over a meal in their home.

All the experiences of the resurrected Jesus were to be given new depth and permanence by the coming of the Holy Spirit at Pentecost, as we will see in the next section. Faith in the risen Christ and the dynamic of the Holy Spirit continue to drive and motivate Christians today. The death of Jesus was not the end. For the disciples many preconceived notions of who Jesus was had to be abandoned. The fear and guilt which had enveloped them at Gethsemane and at the crucifixion had to be left behind.

Meditation

What preoccupations or wrong directions might we have to let go of in order to begin a new kind of life? In what ways does the resurrection of Jesus change the way we look at our future?

Prayer

Risen Lord, help me to make room for you in my life. Give me insight to abandon everything which blinds me to your constant presence. Invigorate me with your resurrection life.   Amen

43 Further resurrection appearances

When the pair from Emmaus reached Jerusalem they shared their experiences with the disciples there, who told them that Peter too had seen Jesus. As they were talking Jesus appeared, greeting them with the words 'Peace be with you.' At first they were all terrified, and thought they were seeing a ghost; but he said: 'Why are you worried and doubtful? Look at my hands and feet and touch me; no ghost has flesh and bones as I do.' He further convinced them by eating a piece of fish. He explained once again how the Scriptures had foretold his sufferings and resurrection, and said that repentance and the forgiveness of sins were to be preached in his name to the whole world. Then he led them to Bethany, blessed them and was parted from them. Full of joy they returned to Jerusalem and praised God daily in the Temple.

One of the apostles, Thomas the Twin, had not been with the others that day, and refused to believe in the resurrection without physical proof. A week later Jesus appeared to the disciples again, and invited Thomas to touch the wounds in his hands and his side. Thomas exclaimed: 'My Lord and my God!' Jesus said to him: 'Because you have seen me you have found faith. Happy are they who find faith without seeing me.'

Some time later a group of disciples, led by Peter, returned to Galilee and spent a fruitless night fishing. When dawn came Jesus was standing at the water's edge. He called to them to make a further cast of the net, and when they did so they made so large a catch that they could not haul the net into the boat. Realising that it was Jesus who had hailed them, Peter plunged into the water to reach him while the others brought the boat ashore.

The disciples breakfasted on food which Jesus had prepared; then he took Peter aside, and three times asked him 'Do you love me?' . Three times Peter replied that he did, and three times Jesus told him: 'Tend my sheep'. Then he promised him a martyr's death.

Jesus did much else which has not been recorded here. These stories have been told in order that you might believe that Jesus is the Son of God, and that through faith in him you may have eternal life.

Luke 24.33-53; John 20.24-21.19

The living presence of Christ

The appearances of the risen Jesus were not limited to a few, deeply grieving, followers in Jerusalem. Paul wrote to the young church at Corinth that over 500 at once saw Jesus after the resurrection.[1]

Each of Jesus' appearances strengthened the reality of what had happened. He points out the physical evidence of his scarred hands and side. He ate with His disciples and linked what was happening to the sacred writings of the scriptures. Jesus was to be present where ever they were – back at work fishing, in their homes, on journeys and wherever they were gathered together.

Perhaps the most encouraging of these encounters was with Thomas. He was bold enough to express doubts and was only satisfied when Jesus spoke to him and he was able to touch Jesus's scars. Sometimes our faith is a struggle which demands the best of our thinking, our emotions and our activity. It will be stronger when doubts have been honestly faced.

The resurrection is central to the whole story of Jesus and from these early times there emerged significant common characteristics in the lives of the local churches and each of these sprang from the resurrection. The resurrection was verified and given authority by reference to the Jewish Scriptures and the sayings of Jesus himself. The message of resurrection was put before the world by preaching. Finally the Risen Lord invited his disciples to a life of love and sacrifice.

Meditation

Living Christian communities still have about them a sharing fellowship, an obedience to scripture, an awareness of God's presence in sacrament and an imperative of mission and service to the world. Such communities believe that the risen Christ is in their midst. These are some of the characteristics we might look for when we think of joining a local church.

Prayer

Risen Lord, give me the faith to recognise your living presence with me wherever I go so that in all things my life may be pleasing to you and I may be guided by your power. Amen

[1] Corinthians 15.6

44 The Ascension, Pentecost and the early Church

The risen Jesus appeared to his friends over forty days. A final meeting took place on the Mount of Olives near Jerusalem; there, having promised them the gift of the Holy Spirit and having commanded them to bear witness to him to the ends of the earth, he ascended into heaven.

During the Jewish feast of Pentecost, which came soon afterwards, the Holy Spirit descended on them in wind and flame, and inspired them to speak in other tongues. People from all over the Mediterranean world who were in Jerusalem during the festival were astonished when they heard them. Peter told the crowd that the prophet Joel had foretold this outpouring of the Holy Spirit, and that Jesus, whom they had crucified, had risen from the dead as Lord and Christ.

Many of Peter's audience joined the infant Christian Church, which grew to be several thousand strong. They shared their possessions and worshipped both in the Temple and in their homes. They soon attracted the attention of the authorities, but their leaders defied injunctions not to speak about Jesus. Warnings gave place to threats and then to floggings, but the Church continued to grow.

The Church appointed seven officers named deacons to look after their poorest members. The preaching of one of them, Stephen, aroused bitter hostility, and he was brought before the Jewish authorities. Replying to the charges against him, he showed how Jesus fitted into the sacred history of the Jews, and accused them of constantly rejecting those whom God had sent them. When he claimed to see Jesus standing at God's right hand he was stoned to death.

A young man called Saul, a devout Pharisee from the city of Tarsus in Asia-Minor, joined enthusiastically in the persecution of Christians. He was sent to Damascus with letters authorising him to arrest any Christians he found there. On his journey a light from heaven flashed around him and he fell to the ground. A voice said: 'Saul, why are you persecuting me?' Saul said: 'Lord, who are you?' The voice replied: 'I am Jesus. Go into the city and you will be told what to do'. When the vision passed Saul found he was blind, and so his companions led him into Damascus. There a Christian named Ananias was told in a vision to visit him. He did so, cured his blindness and conferred the Holy Spirit on him. Saul was baptised, and immediately began to teach that Jesus was the Son of God.

Acts 1.1 - 9.22

The Holy Spirit at work

The experience of the Resurrection of Jesus was followed by the profound awareness of the Holy Spirit in the lives of the disciples. They described this in [1]several ways but whatever happened was clearly life changing. Jesus had promised them this power so that they could fulfil his command to tell the news about him in all the known world.[2]

Two key figures emerged who were to be the leaders of the church and who, arguably, changed the history of the world. The first was Peter, still in Jerusalem and a new man after the experience of Pentecost. Peter was able to link the life and sayings of Jesus to significant passages in the Jewish Scriptures and as a result many Jews became part of the small Christian community in Jerusalem.

The second key figure was Saul, soon to be renamed Paul, after his conversion on the Damascus road. He was a leading Jew himself yet he soon became the indispensable missionary who founded churches in Asia Minor (now Turkey), in Greece and eventually reached Rome to teach the church there.

From the start the expansion of the new Christian church was costly. Many of the Christians, including all the key leaders, were to lose their lives at the hands of Roman Emperors who feared a new religion would usurp their claim to deity and disturb the official, pagan religion of the Roman Empire. The Jewish leaders also remained suspicious of Christians even though many of the first Christians were converted Jews.

Meditation

The early church and its members had a distinctive lifestyle.[3] They listened to teaching in the context of 'breaking bread' and praying together; they shared in a common life together and generously helped each out according to needs. They worshipped both in the Temple and in private houses and they clearly had a lot of fun together. In spite of opposition the churches grew rapidly. It is worth comparing this life style with modern churches and asking what remains and what is missing of that early dynamic.

[1] Acts 2.1-21   [2] Acts 1.8
[3] Acts 2.42-47

45 The Christian Church grows and develops

In ensuing years Christian congregations were set up throughout the eastern Mediterranean. It soon became a burning issue whether Gentiles (non-Jews) could become Christians without becoming Jews as well.

On a missionary tour round some of the new congregations Peter came to Joppa. There he had a vision in which a sheet containing creatures of every description, including those which Jews were forbidden to eat, was lowered from heaven. A voice commanded: 'Get up, Peter, kill and eat!' Peter refused, saying he had never eaten anything unclean. The response came: 'It is not for you to call unclean anything which God calls clean'. While Peter was puzzling over this experience a messenger summoned him to Caesarea, where a devout Roman centurion called Cornelius asked him to speak about his faith. As Peter did so the Holy Spirit descended upon his hearers, all Gentiles. Because of his vision Peter had no hesitation in baptising them.

Meanwhile Saul, now generally known by his Roman name of Paul, based himself in the town of Antioch in Cilicia, and from there undertook missionary journeys to neighbouring lands. His standard practice was to preach first in the local synagogue, to Jews and people who were not Jews but who attended Jewish worship; then, if his ministry was rejected, he left the synagogue and preached only to Gentiles. He was much harassed by those Jews whom he failed to convert; he had to flee from place to place, and on one occasion was stoned and left for dead. Meanwhile the persecution of Christians continued elsewhere. Herod beheaded James the brother of John, and imprisoned Peter, who was preserved only by a miraculous escape from prison.

The admission of Gentiles to the Church remained a contentious topic, and a council was held in Jerusalem to decide what policy should be. The conclusion was that it was not necessary for Christians from a Gentile background to keep the Jewish Law, save in certain minor respects. This decision opened the way for the Church to spread more rapidly still.

On another missionary journey Paul crossed over to the European mainland and evangelised in Greece. In Philippi in Macedonia he and his companion were flogged and imprisoned after Paul had cured a possessed slave-girl. They refused the opportunity to escape which an earthquake afforded, and so impressed the prison governor that he and all his family were baptised.

Acts 9.31 - 16.40

Faith leads to action

It was important for Jews to remain 'clean' by observing Jewish law and not associating with non-Jews. Peter was a Jew and although he had become a believer in Christ, a Christian, he was still anxious to preserve the laws with which he had been brought up.

Jesus came to show all people the way to God. So God sent a strange dream to Peter, but it had a clear message. "It is not for you to call unclean anything which God calls clean." From that Peter understood that God wanted him to speak about his faith to Gentiles as well as Jews. As a result everyone heard about Christ and many became Christians.

Paul meanwhile was having a harder time of it. He saw his work as seeking to reach the Gentiles with the Christian message. He was facing opposition to such an extent that he was once stoned for his words. However Paul was faithful and it wasn't his words which won the prison governor over to faith in Christ, but his actions.

Both Peter and Paul had a story to tell. Their lives had been turned around by their encounter with Jesus Christ. This was such good news for them that they longed to tell others about it.

Meditation

It is often easier to continue to follow old ways and habits. The thought of living our lives in a new way can make us feel anxious and fearful. Jesus said that he is the way, the truth and the life, that no-one comes to God except through him. This is the good news that Paul and Peter had discovered. They made changes to their lives. It was difficult, but God helped them. He was there for them, even in the most testing of circumstances.

Prayer

Dear God, help me to know you are there,
especially in difficult times.

Show me how Jesus may touch my life
and show me the path to you.   Amen

46 Further expansion: Paul's travels

Paul travelled on through Greece, gaining converts and provoking opposition wherever he went. In Athens he was greeted with lively curiosity but made only a few converts. In Corinth the local Jews brought him before the Roman governor Gallio; but Gallio refused to intervene in what he considered to be a dispute within the Jewish community.

Later Paul came to Ephesus in Asia-Minor. His successful ministry there enraged the local silversmiths, whose living came from making statues of the city's deity, Artemis. A serious riot broke out; Paul wanted to speak to the protesters, but, fearing for his safety, the local Christians would not allow it. It was left to a local official to quell the crowd and restore order.

In due course Paul decided to return to Jerusalem, even though he knew that he was putting himself in grave danger; on his way he visited churches which he had established earlier, to say goodbye. In Jerusalem he visited James, the brother of Jesus and head of the church there, and was asked to prove that he still thought of himself as a Jew by undertaking a ritual purification in the Temple. While he was doing so he was recognised and accused of profaning the Jewish faith and the Temple itself. He was rescued from the fury of the mob by a detachment from the Roman garrison; and subsequently from a plot to murder him by being taken to Caesarea. There he was brought before two successive Roman governors, the second of whom asked him to return to Jerusalem and stand trial before a Jewish court. To have agreed would have meant certain death; so Paul took advantage of the fact that he had been born a Roman citizen, and appealed to the Emperor. This meant that he would have to travel as a prisoner to Rome.

The ship on which he and his companions were embarked set sail for Rome, but was caught in a storm and wrecked on the coast of Malta. Thanks to Paul's leadership the crew and passengers all came safely ashore; it was only after some months that he set sail again and came to Rome. He was greeted warmly by the Christians there, and imprisoned in comfortable circumstances to await his trial. Once again most of the local Jews rejected his teaching, and once again he turned to the Gentiles, teaching them without hindrance.

Acts 17 - 28

Paul sticks to his priorities

Have you ever met someone who just seems to attract one disaster after another? Every time you hear from them something else awful has happened. Right now Paul seems to be one of those people.

Travelling in those days needed serious commitment. You either went by foot in sandals, by horseback or by ship, none of it very comfortable or fast. Despite the difficulties however, the good news of Jesus Christ was spreading far and wide. It seems that wherever Paul went he just couldn't help talking about his faith, even though he often knew it would cause problems for him. When we are having a bad day it's good to receive encouragement giving us the stamina we need to get through to the end.

One night whilst Paul was in Corinth the Lord spoke to him in a vision: "Do not be afraid; keep speaking, do not be silent. For I am with you..." [1]

Paul's perseverance came from knowing he was not in this alone, that he was doing the right thing. Even though it was really tough, he had the encouragement he needed to keep going. And others too were on hand to help Paul when he needed it - other Christians, a detachment from the Roman Garrison and even his "passport", his Roman citizenship.

Meditation

God has amazing ways of working in our lives, though often we are too busy to notice. We get bogged down in the here and now, in the trials of the moment. We miss the bigger picture, we miss the encouragement, the people and circumstances which help us get through to the end. Paul ends up here doing what he does best, talking! But his experiences of hardship mean he is speaking with increased wisdom and authority.

Who can I encourage today? Am I so caught up in my problems that I am missing the times of encouragement coming my way?

[1] Acts 18.9

The growing church

Historic Names
(Modern Names)

500 Miles

500 Kms

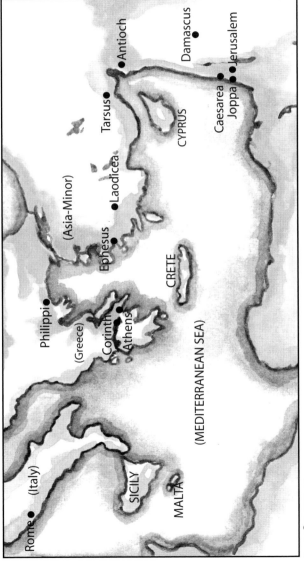

The letters written to congregations and individuals by early Christian leaders guided people in the way of Christ. Paul taught that, ever since the days of Adam, humankind has been inherently sinful. God gave his chosen people, the Jews, the Law as guidance for behaviour and so that sinfulness should become apparent. But a right relationship with God depends, not on trying to keep the Law, but on faith in the saving death of Jesus Christ. Jesus was in the form of God, but for our sake he laid aside his divine attributes and became a humble human being. He lived a life of obedience to the divine will, to the point of dying on the cross. Then he was raised and exalted, and now he reigns in heaven as Lord.

Through Jesus' self-giving love, reconciliation between humankind and God has become possible. All those who have faith and been baptised have received the Holy Spirit, and have entered into a new life, shared with and depending upon the life of Christ. Christians must still wrestle with their old sinful nature; but they can be confident that in the strength of the Holy Spirit they will gradually be transformed into the new people God wishes them to be. After death comes resurrection, when our human, perishable bodies will give place to bodies which are imperishable and immortal.

The Holy Spirit confers gifts on individual Christians. For example, they may be able to teach, to administer, to heal, or to speak in tongues. Each gift enables its recipient to play a part in the Church, which is the body of Christ, continuing his work on earth. The Spirit also bears fruit in individual lives, producing such virtues as love, joy, peace, patience, kindness, goodness, fidelity, gentleness and self-control.

The greatest gift is love. Love is patient and kind; envies no-one and is neither boastful nor conceited; is never rude, selfish or quick to take offence. Love does not count up grievances or take pleasure in the failings of others. Love's joy is in the truth: there is no limit to its faith, hope and endurance.

The letter to the Hebrews explains Jesus' significance in another way, using a metaphor based on the Jewish sacrificial system. Jesus is the great high priest, entering the Holy of Holies to offer the perfect sacrifice of himself. The old sacrifices could not take away sin and needed constant repetition, but Christ's sacrifice takes away sin once and for all.

Romans, 1 Corinthians; Galatians; Philippians; Hebrews

Understanding and living the Christian faith

Paul spent much of his time travelling around new churches, teaching new converts. Now that they had become Christians, Paul helped them to understand that having a right relationship with God means having a relationship of faith with Christ, not just following the Law. For the Jews this was radical teaching, but for those who chose to believe, it was a new freedom.

Paul was once a teacher of the Jewish faith. He knew of the frustrations of trying to keep every minute requirement of the Law. Whenever people think they can simply pull themselves together and then they will be able to do everything rightly and well, it leads to disappointment. We need a stronger motivation to change than simply keeping to a ritual code.

That's where our relationship with Christ comes in. It is that which lifts us above merely satisfying ourselves or appearing good to others. Our longing is to respond fully to the love Christ offers us. That is the thrust of Paul's teaching especially to those who think they can improve their own standing and rightness before God in their own strength. Love for and obedience to Christ is the motivation of a truly Christian life.

Through the Holy Spirit, we learn how to use our gifts and skills for the benefit of others and for the building up of the Church. If we do this we not only bless others, but receive blessing ourselves – often in surprising ways. As we give to others we find our own desires and needs fulfilled in wonderful ways.

Meditation

There must be more to Christianity that being a respectable citizen. The early Christians, and many who have followed them, had a passion for Christ and a strong desire for others to follow Him. Where can you see that fire in Christians today?

The young Church: difficulties

As Christianity spread, and as non-Jews joined the church in large numbers, many problems arose. Paul addressed some of them in his letters.

In Corinth the church had divided into parties, each claiming a prominent Christian as its leader. Paul pointed out that the Church had only one true leader - Christ - and that unity in Christ was essential. So was mutual respect. Christians were variously gifted, but no one gift was more important than another. All were essential for building up the Church, the body of Christ.

There were sometimes questions about finance. While Paul paid his own way, he thought that apostles had a right to support from the churches they served. He also thought local churches should look beyond themselves to the needs of others. He organised a collection on behalf of the church in Jerusalem, which had fallen upon hard times, and encouraged churches far and wide to contribute to it.

Paul believed that the Christian community should resolve disagreements among its members without resort to the secular courts. Those guilty of sexual immorality should be disciplined. While celibacy was admirable, it was not for everybody. Marriage, through which a man and a woman became one flesh, was the only right way of expressing sexuality physically. Marriage should be permanent; it was only when a believing and an unbelieving partner could not agree to live together that separation should occur.

It was difficult for Christians to decide how far they should separate themselves from the practices of their pagan neighbours when they spilled over into daily life. Paul's advice was that there was nothing intrinsically wrong in, for example, eating meat which had been offered to an idol; but the first priority was to do nothing which might hurt other Christians who thought differently.

The religious meals of the Corinthian church, held, as were all early meetings for worship, in private houses, had degenerated because the food families brought had not been shared, and the poor had been left hungry. Paul taught that the Lord's Supper should be a communal meal, and that the act of worship should derive from the words of Jesus at the Last Supper. Worship should not be dominated by speaking in tongues, but should also include prayer, prophecy and hymn-singing, with leadership widely shared among the men present.

1 and 2 Corinthians

Living lives consistent with our beliefs

Corinth was a major city in the time of Paul; travellers and traders passed through daily and two harbours ensured a busy, cosmopolitan city. Corinth, however, was also known for its immorality and the new Christian believers were struggling in this setting. Congregations split as disagreements uncovered a lack of unity and new believers were pulled back towards the pagan lifestyles of those around them.

Into this setting Paul speaks up for the good news of Jesus Christ. He is like the anchor for a ship that is being tossed about by the wind. He deals with each of the situations with patience and wisdom. He points out that Christians should live lives that are honest financially, relationally and spiritually. Christians should be generous and take care of one another. Disagreements should be resolved between themselves. There should be purity in marriage which should be a permanent relationship between a man and a woman. In other words, these new believers were to live lives that were demonstrably different to the lives of those around them. Their lives should reflect the teachings of Christ lived out for all to see.

Our cities today are not so very different from Corinth in the time of Paul. It is not hard to be pulled away from living the kind of life Paul encourages the Corinthians to live. We have pressure from family, friends, colleagues and the accepted standards of society that persuades us that living our lives in contradiction to the Bible is not a problem. We only have to look around us to see the mess that selfish living causes.

Paul refocuses the Corinthians back to Christ. When we lose sight of Jesus' example in our lives, we lose the anchor we need.

Meditation

Where in my life do I need to refocus on Christ? Are there issues in today's society which run contrary to the teachings of Christ and which demand that I stand up and be counted as a follower of him? Can I name those issues which cause me concern?

The letters written by Paul and others contain much practical advice about how Christians, living in a world which was often uncomprehending and hostile, should conduct themselves in daily life.

They were to abstain from foolish and damaging speech; from drunkenness and dissipation; from coarse and flippant talk; from envy and contention; from anger and selfish ambition; from greed and from retaliation for harm done to them; from sexual relations outside marriage. They were to be patient under persecution. The wealthy among them were to remember the impermanence of riches, to repent of their misuse, and to be generous in well-doing. They were to fill their minds with thoughts which were true, noble, just, pure, loving, attractive, excellent and admirable.

Christians were to regard every other Christian, no matter what his or her status or background, as a brother or sister, equally entitled to respect, love, and care in times of need. They were to be tolerant of disagreements about religious practice. They were to be peaceable citizens, praying for their rulers and being obedient to authority. Men should love their wives in the same way that Christ loves his Church, and treat their children and their slaves with justice and kindness. Wives should be obedient to their husbands and modest in their appearance and behaviour; children and slaves should be obedient and diligent. Generous hospitality was a duty.

Paul illustrated the Christian life in action in a letter to his Christian friend Philemon. One of Philemon's slaves, Onesimus, had run away, had met Paul and had become a Christian. Paul sent him back to Philemon, asking him to forgive Onesimus' offences and to receive him as a brother.

Above all, the Christian life should be infused with love. Christians should love each other because God is love. God showed his love by sending his Son as a sacrifice for our sins, in order to give us eternal life. Christians know that they live in him and he in them because he has given his Holy Spirit to them. The gift and the seal of the Spirit is love; anyone who lives in love lives in God, and God lives in him. Love does away with the fear of judgment; but anyone who claims to love God while hating a fellow-Christian is deceiving himself. Whoever loves God must love his fellow-Christians too.

Romans; Ephesians; Philippians; 1 Timothy;
James; 1 Peter; Philemon; 1 John

Creating a Christian culture

If you have had the experience of moving to another country you will understand the difficulties of learning to live in a new culture. Expectations of dress, hospitality, friendships, business methods and, not least, language, are all a minefield of potential social disaster.

The new Christians Paul was teaching were experiencing something similar. Although they had not moved to a new country, they had moved from a pagan culture to a new way of living as believers in Christ. These days we might try and understand how we should behave in a new culture by reading about it on the internet or in books. But best of all is to talk to somebody who has lived in that culture and who can tell you how you might understand I and seek to adapt to it.

This is what Paul was doing. He was a Christian with experience of living like one and so he shared with others about how to live in a Christian culture. There are new ways of behaving such as treating everyone as spiritual equals, regardless of status or background. In a society which had slaves and masters this was astonishing teaching; but in Christ all are equal and worthy. Paul encourages his hearers to be generous with money, hospitality and brotherly love. When we feel like hating we must love, when we feel like lying we must tell the truth, when someone hurts us, we must forgive them.

However, Christians are unable to live new lives in their own strength without reference to God. God is love and it is by his Holy Spirit that Christians receive the strength needed to live lives often at odds with the world around them. Living a Christian life puts others first with Christ at the centre.

Meditation

If, in today's world, Christians may have to swim against the tide of popular culture, there are ways in which they can support each other. When we feel isolated the local church or the internet may offer some leads to other Christians who have the same concerns as you do.

Prayer

Dear God, help me to live with you in my heart and others in my thoughts and give strength to be true to Christ's teaching. Amen

50 Revelation

A Christian named John, in exile on the Mediterranean island of Patmos, wrote about a series of visions granted to him. He saw the risen Jesus, and was entrusted by him with messages to seven churches in Asia-Minor. The messages comforted the churches in their affliction and praised them for their virtues; but they also contained sharp criticisms of respects in which they had fallen short. For example, the church at Laodicea was criticised for being lukewarm in its devotion and complacent in its prosperity. The message went on: 'Behold, I stand knocking at your door. If anyone opens the door I will come in and he and I will eat together.'

John's visions turned to the heavenly court where God the Father sat enthroned in glory and honour, surrounded by creatures both human and not, and receiving unending hymns of praise. With him stood the Lamb (that is, Jesus) who, by opening a scroll, loosed dreadful disasters on the earth; only the true servants of God were exempt, with special honour being accorded to those who had died as martyrs. Further visions of judgment followed, culminating in a prophecy that Rome, the great Babylon, would be utterly destroyed. All this was part of a cosmic struggle between the forces of good and evil, which ended with the Devil being defeated and cast into an everlasting lake of fire. All humankind was judged, and those whose names were not found in the book of life were cast into the lake of fire too.

Then a new heaven and a new earth emerged. The Holy City, a new Jerusalem, came down from heaven. It needed no temple because God was fully present there; nor did it need the sun or moon because of the divine light which pervaded it. Through the city flowed the river of the water of life; and within it God's servants saw him and the Lamb face to face for ever.

The visions ended with Jesus saying: 'Let the thirsty come; let whoever so desires receive the water of life. Yes, I am coming soon'; and John responding: 'Amen! Come, Lord Jesus.'

Revelation

Jesus the Victor!

John the Divine, as he has become known, wrote for his own time and for all time. He wrote for the churches of his time and seven of them in particular. He had a manner of writing with which his readers would be familiar but which nowadays we find strange and difficult. It is called apocalyptic and has strong echoes of some Old Testament writings, especially the writings of prophets like Ezekiel and Daniel. The writing is visionary, highly symbolised and weaves to and fro amongst its themes.

He wrote at a time when many believed that the end of the world was very near and judgement was at hand. Yet none of his predictions came about in John's own time as he expected: Rome was not overthrown for centuries; the end of the world did not come and supernatural terrors failed to appear in the time and place he predicted.

But John wrote for all time as well. We think of time as linear and what began must sometime end as opposed to a loop of events coming round again and again. John's vision is that what began with the creation of God must end with the vindication of the Creator. Good triumphs over evil, despotic emperors are overthrown, cities become perfect and holy and God's judgement is carried out.

We are therefore left with John's great convictions to inspire us in the ongoing conflict between good and evil. The epic story of God's relationship with humankind concludes in a crescendo of glory and power and victory for the One who sits on the throne. He presides over a kingdom where peace is enjoyed, justice is vindicated and the Holy God rules in glory. The picture of splendour and light is made all the more glorious because it has been achieved by Christ who met the worst of evil in the world and won a great victory over it.

Prayer

Almighty God I sing praises to your majesty and glory,

Lord Jesus I give you thanks for your victory over evil,

Holy Spirit draw me into the presence and splendour
of the living God,

Father Son and Holy Spirit, bless me now and evermore.

Amen